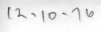

12-10-76

12-10-76

Stay With Us, Lord

Joseph Manton, C.SS.R.

Our Sunday Visitor, Inc.
Huntington, Indiana 46750

Other books by Father Manton:
PENNIES FROM A POORBOX
STRAWS FROM THE CRIB
SANCTITY ON THE SIDE WALK
HAPPINESS OVER THE HILL

Imprimi Potest:
Very Rev. Joseph L. Kerins, C.SS.R.,
Provincial

Nihil Obstat:
Rev. Lawrence Gollner
Censor Librorum

Imprimatur:
✠Leo A. Pursley, D.D.
Bishop of Fort Wayne-South Bend
April 25, 1974

The Nihil Obstat and Imprimatur are official declarations that a book or pamphlet is free of doctrinal or moral error. No implication is contained therein that those who have granted the Nihil Obstat or Imprimatur agree with the contents, opinions or statements expressed.

ISBN: 0-87973-786-7
Library of Congress Catalog Card Number: 74-028505

Cover Design by James E. McIlrath

Published, printed and bound in the U.S.A. by
Our Sunday Visitor, Inc.
Noll Plaza,
Huntington, Indiana 46750
786

Contents

Saints, Incorporated

Thoughts on the feast of All Saints should accent the *all*. On some days the Church commemorates one saint, on another two, or on some days three or more, as with a group of martyrs. Thus one feast day is a solo, and the next may be a duet, and the following day a trio. All Saints Day, the first of November, is the great swelling chorus of *all* the saints together.

But note this: All Saints Day is not devoted exclusively to the officially canonized saints. After all, they have their own feast days. On All Saints Day we honor that vast uncanonized, unrecognized, unnumbered multitude of saints that nobody ever heard of; for example, probably your own deceased mother and father. For who is a saint? Anyone who has died in the friendship of God. Anyone who may have sinned, but who has repented, and has been reconciled, and who finally passed away at peace with his Maker.

It is true that these people may not have been saints of towering holiness. In the same way the foothills of the Catskills are not the Alps or the Andes, they still are hills and not hollows. And these lower, lesser people who are in heaven are saints and not reprobates in hell.

The feast of All Saints belongs particularly to them, not to St. Francis of Assisi or to St. Anthony of Padua or

to St. Theresa of Lisieux. It's the day for some anonymous St. Mary of Milwaukee, or some unrecognized St.
Alice of Albany, or some obscure St. Henry of Hacken-
sack. Their halos were perhaps the eye-reflector of a surgeon, the pert white cap of a nurse, the scarred helmet of
a fireman, or the rumpled dust-cap of a housewife.

Some of them, in the catalogue of the saints, might
be set down as hermits, only their cells were lonely
rooms in the great wilderness of a sullen, hostile city.
Others were martyrs, not bound to a glowing gridiron
like St. Lawrence, but standing and bending, red faced
and weary, at their daily tasks. All of them were apostles
or preachers of the gospel. Their churches were little
corners of the world, where their silent sermons thun-
dered over and over again one glorious text, namely, the
quiet example of the good life they lived for God without
thought of making any impression on anybody.

These were saints whose sky never exploded with
skyrocketing bursts of spectacular miracles. These were
the saints who led lives as dull and prosaic as car tracks,
but, like the car tracks, straight and on the level and
true. These were the people who felt the sting of insult
and the slight of being ignored, but who did not grow bitter or sulk nor did they retaliate with venomous spite.
The people who at times were down in health and often
low in spirit, but who never despaired. The people who
sometimes felt that God was vague and far off, but who
still looked up to Him and hoped. The ones who were
brave when there was no audience to see, and loyal when
there was no reward in sight. The ones who knew that
life was a hard road under a hot sun, but who still plodded toward the distant goal. The ones who sometimes
fell — into sin — but who grimly picked themselves up,
brushed off the dirt, and pushed on with sparks of new
determination glinting in their eyes.

These are the people we talk about and think about
on All Saints Day. When alive, they got no recognition.
Even the worldly world pauses at the shrine of the saint
who *cured* sickness with miraculous power; but even the

Christian world passes by the men and women who merely *endured* sickness with miraculous patience. The world lays its wreaths at the tombs of great conquerors like Napoleon and Alexander the Great; God lays His rose upon the grave of the man who has fought and conquered his rebellious passions upon the swaying battlefield of the soul.

The world writes books about great sculptors like Michelangelo, but it seldom speaks about or even hears about the Christian mother and father who so carefully molded the beautiful character of a child. All Saints Day reminds us that the world is flooded with counterfeit ideas and ideals, but the man or woman who is not taken in by them, who is not lured off his course by the bright lights of the world's pleasure, but who steers his course by the north star of the Church and faith, who keeps the passport of his soul clean and ready because at any day he may find himself at the custom borders of eternity — this is the man or the woman who may be sitting alongside us at a cafeteria or standing next to us in a crowded bus, and whose feast — believe it or not — we may be celebrating next year on the Feast of All Saints.

At this moment God, of course, knows them all. He knows, for example, young Kevin, just turned twenty, who wears the white plume of a clean soul in a mud-spattered world. He knows Aunt Martha, who has been bent almost double with arthritis these many years, and whose body is an altar of sacrifice from which she offers each day's pain to the crucified Christ. He knows the quiet and dedicated Dorothy, who a decade ago dreamed of orange blossoms and organ music, but ever since has spent her days amid the buzzes and flashes of a switchboard to keep a home for her widowed invalid mother.

This same God knows the Schneiders, the McDonnells, and the Lombardis whose homes are empty of luxuries but filled with a deep inner happiness; families who have not been able to open the door to the man with the latest model color television or dish-washing machine, but who have never closed that door upon the will of God. This God knows that smiling grandmother at whose casket I knelt and prayed. She raised her family and went on to grow weak and old. Her hearing began to fail and she needed a hearing-aid; her eyes grew dim and the world became a misty blur; her toes had to come off because of a diabetic condition, and after that the grim amputation of both legs. . . .

Meanwhile this incredible woman with towering courage and soaring faith wore out three wheel chairs. Can you imagine that she was one of the people poised at her radio every week to whom I and priests like me had the nerve to preach? Now that she has died, does anyone doubt that she is in heaven? Can there be any question that this is her feast day. All Saints?

All Saints Day is the day of recognition and reward for the common Christian. It is the day that should start the bells of happiness and the chimes of hope swinging in every Catholic heart. Down from the battlements of heaven come the smiles of those who have gone before us. They have made it; we can do the same! This is the triumphant call that comes ringing down to us, because, poor wavering sinners though we be, if we do not give up, if we go on with courage in our hearts, with God's grace in our souls, we can look forward to All Saints Day as our feast day too!

There is a time in the year when the papers carry a list of names and the pictures of a few smiling faces — the happy people who have passed the bar and have been admitted to the practice of law. Try to imagine the over-whelming joy of those who have made it to a far higher goal; those who have made it for the eternal joy of heaven! These are the saints. Someone has described them as those who were agreeable, when they wanted to be disagreeable; who kept silent, when they wanted to blurt out; who kept on going, when they wanted to quit. The *trick* is to persevere, day after day and year after year. The *treat* is heaven.

The saints never were made of pious plaster. They were people. They were not quitters. No quitter ever got his name in the Litany of the Saints. Their motto was *excelsior* (higher), and their chief characteristic was rugged determination. Quit is a four-letter word, and alas, so is hell. Heaven is something more.

Saints of the Calloused Hands

Once St. Joseph had brought the Child and His Mother back from Egypt, and settled in placid Nazareth, it would have been hard for even a Madison Avenue advertising agency to drape his drab life with glamor and excitement. If you demand a pageant of color or the thrill of adventure in your saints, switch to another channel. Joseph is not for you. You might try some one like St. Benedict. Now there was drama: Benedict, sitting down to dine with his monks, and among them a few malcontents who eyed the sinister goblet at the abbot's place. It contained poison. But when the saint blesses his meal, as is his wont, the goblet shatters and the death drink spills harmlessly on the monastery board.

Or you might turn to someone like St. Vincent de Paul, straining at his long oar in the prison galley while the jailer's whip curled across his sweating shoulders. Or consider St. Joan of Arc, mounted on a white horse and gleaming in her silver armor, riding off to battle amid bright lances and fluttering banners. These saints did have color, and movies were made of their lives. If they tried that with St. Joseph, there would be nothing on the sound track but the drone of a saw and the swish of a plane, and scenes about as colorful as an old plank or a pile of sawdust.

Still, in terms of rank none of these saints is in the same league with St. Joseph. They are like young interns, while he is chief of surgery. Never was so lofty a post as foster-father of the Redeemer joined to so lowly a station as village carpenter.

It is ironic, but also characteristic, that after St. Lawrence men have named a mighty river; after St. Louis a great city; after St. James a splendid palace; after St. Bernard a huge dog; but after St. Joseph an aspirin. Spiritual writers try to make up by presenting him as one of the holy trinity of earth: Jesus, Mary, Joseph; but even there, had you got to meet him, he would have probably had to lay down an oily tool, put out a grimy hand, and stand there a bit self-conscious like any toil-stained workingman.

Somebody wrote a poem once (I can neither quote verse nor cite author) about Joseph on the road to Bethlehem, as he held the bridle of Mary's plodding mule. Suddenly he hears behind him the whirring clatter of swift wheels, and nudges the beast to the side of the road in time to let a Roman chariot, all gilded and handsome, go flashing by, while the proud owner curses this awkward peasant for cluttering the road. Poor Joseph can only catch his breath as the yellow dust chokes his throat and smarts his eyes.

Is it allowed to wonder at this late date, who was the important personage hurrying to such pressing business of state, or to the social event of the season? All we can be sure of now is that he was racing in style to oblivion, while Joseph was humbly plodding on to immortality. Each Christmas the world remembers Joseph and Mary on the Bethlehem road. The gaze of God was on them then, and is still on all those who walk the road of life in their spirit.

If that charioteer disdainfully ignored St. Joseph, let us admit that the Church also waved him into the shadows for many hundreds of years. Those were the times of an illiterate peasantry who, if they continually heard about Jesus, Mary and Joseph, might naturally assume that Joseph was the natural father of Jesus. So in the beginning only the Madonna and Child went up in the churchs' stained-glass windows or on oil paintings. After the Middle Ages, when the biblical titles of Mother and Virgin had been firmly set on Our Lady's brow like a double coronet, the Church beckoned St. Joseph back into the spotlight and saluted him with the honors he deserved.

Or rather it was the people. Once they got to know about this obscure, ordinary workman who hammered and sawed his way to sanctity, the common people canonized him. They raised him over their altars and they took him into their hearts. Their argument was simplicity itself: if Joseph had been so close to Christ on earth, must he not be very near to Him and very dear to Him in heaven?

Besides, Joseph like themselves was simply a worker, not a miracle worker. There is no word in the Gospels of any wonder wrought by him. Instead, he merely labored all the day long. Come to think of it, Jesus for most of His life did that too. Is there any facet of the life of Christ more incredible? He postponed the redemption of the world for thirty years while he worked in a village carpenter shop. Was he quietly telling us about the dignity of honest toil? Blessed indeed is that work where we can think of ourselves as laboring between Jesus and Joseph! The thought will turn into an altar any desk, or stove, or operating table, or factory machine.

But for Joseph it was more than work. It was trouble in an endless chain, like a conveyor belt. In the very beginning heaven left him in the dark even while he saw his wife pregnant. Then the grim journey to Bethlehem for that foolish census when the weather was at its worst, and Mary was in her heaviest month. After that the dash toward Egypt to escape the slaughterers of the Holy Innocents. Not to speak of other things, like his sacrifice in renouncing fatherhood, so dear to all Jewish men of that time; plus the responsibility of watching over the most precious Mother and Son this world had ever seen, an assignment more grave than guarding any crown jewels; and the strain of providing his little family with food and clothing. Is there any wonder that St. Joseph came to be the saint invoked by people who had to reach heaven over the rocky road of rent and groceries, sickness and taxes, and all the relentless rest?

Because St. Joseph carried the burdens of the common man, he has pity for him. St. Joseph was so close to the God-man, he has power to help the common man. How close was Joseph to Jesus? In our day the President is guarded by Secret Service men. When they suggest, he obeys. In a similar way Joseph guarded the Child Jesus, and Jesus obeyed him. Later they worked shoulder to shoulder in the carpenter shop. Our whole devotion to St. Joseph rests on the manly love that linked their hearts then, and on the influence that a whispered request from Joseph has now upon the Savior, who for so many years ate at Joseph's table and slept under Joseph's roof.

Ever since St. Teresa claimed that when she prayed to St. Joseph she never drew a blank, his cult has grown. Perhaps heaven, to make up for long centuries when St. Joseph had sat in a dark corner of history wrapped in his unassuming cloak, now lets him send down favors like pieces of gold spilling out of a tilted treasure chest. People invoke some saints in particular areas, but St. Joseph seems to be general delivery.

Is it about a job? They remember that St. Joseph was a workingman himself. Is it about a house? Joseph had his share of house-hunting from Bethlehem to Egypt. Is it some anxiety that cannot be disclosed? The diary of those days and nights when Joseph wondered about the pregnancy of Mary was written in the deep lines across his forehead. Is it even a broken heart? If on earth he was the saint who mended the boy Jesus' broken toys, perhaps from heaven he can put together even a sadly broken heart.

Surely it is only fancy, but it is pleasant to imagine

that each day when the twilight drew down its rose-
colored shades in the west, and Joseph walked wearily
home from his carpenter shop, the Child Jesus was there
to swing open the cottage gate and welcome him with
eyes spilling over with happiness and love. May it be
with us too, when life's long day is over and our weary
work is done, that St. Joseph may be standing there at
the gate of heaven to welcome us to that larger "holy
family," the bright company of the blessed!

The Other Paul

Perhaps we Redemptorists are more attracted to St. Paul of the Cross than to most saints because the religious body he founded, the Passionists, is so close in purpose and spirit to our own. Even our uniform, which is basically a black cassock, is similar to theirs. The main difference is that while the Passionist wears over his heart a white monogram like a varsity letter (they all made the team, all good men!), the Redemptorist wears round his neck a white linen band, perhaps to conceal any roughnecks among us. Anyone who ever tries to attach one of these collars to the cassock with a dozen straight pins, and still achieves a smooth effect, knows which religious order got the better of the deal between the collar and the monogram.

If you put any stock in astrology (which I hope you don't) you might ponder the coincidence that the Passionists and the Redemptorists were born under the same sign of the zodiac. At least at the very time when St. Paul of the Cross was founding the Passionists in the north of Italy, St. Alphonsus was getting the Redemptorists off the launching pad in the south. Genoa was the home base for St. Paul; Naples for St. Alphonsus. Each founder, with tears in his eyes, saw almost all his first disciples pack off and leave him. Each founded an organization of priests and brothers whose lives were to be divided between being monks at home and apostles abroad, moving parish to parish to preach missions.

Eighteenth century Italy was dedicated to an art that was all scarlet and gold and to a pulpit oratory where the ideal sermon was a greenhouse of rhetorical flowers and a museum of classical allusion. St. Paul and St. Alphonsus broke with this absurd tradition and laid it on the line that their missionaries should preach a sermon as simple as a stone and as direct as a hammered nail. Each founder felt he was called by God to bring the Gospel to souls that had been abandoned, to people who were Catholics only in name, to the neglected poor of the back country, to the forgotten peasants in all the Bethlehems of the world.

For St. Paul of the Cross these abandoned souls were at first the charcoal burners living on the edge of the forests. For St. Alphonsus they were the goatherds in the rugged hills. With such a wild background it is no surprise that each of them encountered bandits. St. Alphonsus was shocked to learn that his bandits actually lit votive lights before a picture of the Madonna and prayed that Our Lady would send rich travelers to their ambush. St. Paul went that even one better by being kidnapped himself by bandits, and being carried off into the woods to hear a dying brigand's confession. They could have saved themselves the trouble, of course, if they had merely asked him to come to their hideout for a sick call. But saints have always been mysteries to bandits and vice versa.

Experiences like these would make Paul and Alphonsus eventually smile, but both of them also had plenty of reasons in the course of their lives to weep. Each was misunderstood and misjudged by a reigning Pope. Each was reported to Rome for being lax in the confessional. Their mutual feast could have been the Ascension, because if our Lord went up to heaven under a cloud, Alphonsus and Paul of the Cross for a considerable time lived under one.

Their early lives were somewhat similar. When one was plain Don Alfonso Liguori and the other Paolo Danei in the dashing world of attractive young manhood, zealous relatives tried to marry each of them off; however, neither wanted the golden ring of matrimony but reached out for the golden chalice of priesthood. Not immediately. At first Alphonsus became a lawyer, and Paul joined the army. It was not that Paul especially coddled to soldiering, but at that particular moment in history the infidel Turks were massing for a grand attack on Christian Europe. The Pope sent out a ringing plea for swords around the cross, lest civilization be caught between the cruel horns of the crescent.

The Turkish attack never materialized. After weary months of monotonous waiting the danger petered out. Paul decided he would return home. Apparently enlistments were less technical and more casual in those days. But in the army Paul had seen enough of the seamier side of life to pity his messmates, and now he determined to recruit his own company to fight a fiercer war, a life-long campaign against the devil. He had seen at first hand how vivid and strong temptation could be, and he wanted to form a religious order whose members would see that God got equal time, and who would show men that God's laws, His rewards, and His punishments were even more real and more forceful than the realities of life.

The ancient adage maintains that all beginnings are hard. The founding of the Passionists turned out to be an obstacle course whose architect must have been one of Satan's chief engineers. Even Paul of the Cross might have given up, were it not for the encouragement of his brother, John, who deserves more credit than he generally gets. It is a curiosity of history that among the Twelve Apostles there were three sets of brothers, but it is doubtful if any of these pairs was closer than Paul and his brother John. Both were brothers in blood and in the religious life. Were it not for John's energy and enthusiasm and unfailing confidence, the Passionists might never have become the glorious regiment they became in the army of the Church. Privately, Paul of the Cross confided more than once that his brother John was the holiest man he had ever known, but even he had to admit that John's was a kind of fierce, barbed-wire holiness. Never was a man more aptly named, John the Baptist, because he was as outspoken as a machine gun and had no more idea of compromise than does a traffic light.

Paul, on the other hand, was much kindlier in his makeup. In fact the bishop of the place was so impressed by Paul's quiet sanctity that he asked him to preach a triduum in the town church even before he was ordained. But whenever the occasion required it, Paul could be as forthright as the best of them, and on this occasion he blazed away like a gun battery so that the townspeople brought all their playing cards and dice and carnival costumes and obscene pictures to the public square for a huge bonfire. The ghost of Savanarola must have smiled.

Other people, in other matters, were not so easy to persuade. When Paul of the Cross journeyed to Rome to seek papal approbation for his new religious order (he called them "Barefooted Clerks of the Most Holy Cross"), he could get no farther than the huge iron gate guarding the grounds before the Pope's Quirinal Palace. The tall officer in the blazing uniform and the plumed hat took one look at the scrawny young man in the patched black cassock and the bare feet, and bade him be on his way or he would fling him into jail.

St. Alphonsus could have sympathized with Paul. By the time the Redemptorists were officially approved, St. Alphonsus found himself excluded from his own order. That's another story. It is sad enough to remember that it took all of twenty tormented years from the time that St. Paul of the Cross first sketched out a rough draft of the Passionist Rule, till the finished document was stamped with the approving seal of the Pope. It is not generally known that according to this rule the Passionists take a fourth vow in addition to the usual

ones of poverty, chastity and obedience. The fourth is a
vow to keep constantly before the mind of men our Savior's passion and death. The brothers of the order do this
simply and quietly by wearing on their cassock the Passionist shield, which is the Sacred Heart with the cross
above and nails below, and the abbreviated inscription
"The Passion of Jesus Christ."

The priests keep Christ's passion before the people
chiefly by preaching on it. For them each parish mission
is the huge easel on which they set their glowing word-
paintings of Calvary, which once was the price of sin and
ever since has been the motive to avoid it. Superb ora-
tors that so many Passionists are, it is doubtful if they
ever produced a more direct and powerful missionary
than their founder and spiritual father. When St. Paul
took his place on the platform that characterizes Passionist missions, alongside the tall, gaunt cross, with his
voice sounding like a trumpet, with his sensitive face
changing like sun and shadow on a craggy mountain,
with all the dramatic instincts of an actor, and with a
burning faith blazing like a halo of supernatural power
behind him, it is no wonder that sparks seem to leap
from the pulpit and touch off fires in the hearts of his
hearers in the pews.

Often the large crowds, that came to listen, had to
be diverted from the church to the public square so that
all could be accommodated. Granted that in Italy of the
seventeen-hundreds, people were less sophisticated and
that popular preachers were like spiritual matinee idols
who took the place of theatre and television in a humdrum life, it does not explain the unique magnetism of a
man who would often speak for two solid hours. It is
curious, too, that soldiers especially were attracted to his
sermons, and many of them testified that they never felt
half so frightened in the fiercest battle as when St. Paul
of the Cross took them on a personally conducted tour of
hell.

He was seventy-five years old when he preached his
last mission and had to be helped into the pulpit. Even

at this distant date it makes a touching scene. The weather-beaten veteran of the sanctuary with his crown of white hair, leaned on his staff and pointed a long accusing finger like a district attorney. He pleaded with men to put the saving of their souls before all else, pleading with the persuasion of a man who himself already stood with one foot in eternity. That last sermon must have been something men remembered as long as they lived, particularly when so soon afterward the preacher died.

What had disappointed Paul in his last few years of preaching was that he had become hard of hearing, and had to give up trying to hear confessions because people were reluctant to shout their sins even to a saint. But as long as his eloquent sermons shook the tree, there were many willing priestly hands to gather up the fallen fruit.

If deafness made him cup his hand to his ear, arthritis now made him shuffle along with a cruelly bent back. Once again we think how his life was a carbon copy of St. Alphonsus, who was an arthritic also, and we shake our heads sadly as these two grand old men of God, in parallel wheelchairs, roll off into the twilight together. Young men dream dreams and old men see visions, and it is on record that each of these in his own way stared across the shimmering sea of the future and saw a tall new ship bearing down. St. Alphonsus predicted at the very time when his little band of Redemptorists was only a tiny smoldering fire about to be stamped out by political heels, that his order would burst into glorious flame beyond the Alps. And it happened.

St. Paul of the Cross made a bolder prophecy. One day his Passionists would preach in the least Catholic country of Europe, the heretical England that in those years was hostile to the Church to the point of hatred. That Paul was right in his prediction was proved when one of his spiritual grandsons, Father Dominic, a little Passionist who spoke broken English with a heavy Italian accent, received into the Church one of the great masters of the English language, and one of the most renowned churchmen of the century, John Henry Cardinal Newman.

In America they were muttering about the Stamp Act when St. Paul of the Cross died. It was October 18, 1775. He had just received Viaticum, and as he lay upon his thin straw pallet he asked that a rope be looped round his neck as a sign that a sinner was going to meet his Judge. It sounds melodramatic to us, but each nation marches to its own drum, and he was probably trying to dilute the adulation that whispered "saint" around his deathbed. He asked that one of the monks read him the Passion of Christ from the Gospel of St. Luke, and during the reading he died. It was his eighty-first year. From one end of Italy to the other the cry went up, "Il Santo!" The bright and blessed company of heaven had a new saint. At the official canonization, a little more than a century ago, more than one hundred thousand people filled St. Peter's and overflowed into the great square.

As with any saint, there are strange things recorded in his life which make the ordinary mortal raise a wondering eyebrow. Who, for example, could ever identify with Paul, the cranky child, who would instantly stop his baby tantrums when anyone pointed to the crucifix? Who can feel snugly at home with Paul, the mystic, who was so on fire with love for God that he had to lay his fevered head on the cooling marble of the communion rail? Who is on the same wave length with Paul, the miracle worker, who raised his crucifix over the storm-pelted vineyard so that at the tempest's end the driving hail had stripped every leaf but had left the grapes firm and untouched?

All this is the supernatural, and we who live so much in a world framed by only the superficial, can but stand afar off and marvel. But there is another St. Paul of the Cross to whom it is easy to relate. When he says, "If there is any good in me at all, I owe it to my mother," we feel that here is a man with whom we can be at home. When he looks back on his life and says, "If I had to do it all over again, I would go through the world preaching the mercy of God," we recognize a saint whom we like and love.

Gratefully we salute him in the vesper anthem of his feast:

O Paul, Hunter of souls,
Herald of the Gospel, Pillar of Light,
You learned wisdom from the Wounds of Christ,
You were strengthened for your mission by the Blood of
    Christ,
You led whole towns to repentance through the Suffer-
    ings of Christ,
Receive now your crown from the Hands of Christ!

His Middle Name Was Mary

Amid the rainbow shower of Christmas mail that reaches the rectory each December, there once came a flamboyant card "wishing you and all the other Jesuits at the Mission Church a Most Happy Christmas." Now the priests at the Mission Church happen to be Redemptorists, quite another network, but possibly the writer vaguely remembered from his history how Bismarck, the Iron Chancellor of Germany's Kulturkampf, had demanded the expulsion of all Redemptorists as being "the very worst kind of Jesuits."

Or perhaps he had read somewhere of that charming scene back in the seventeenth century when a Jesuit priest named Father Francis Jerome held in his black-robed arms a chubby Italian infant, looked down into those velvet brown eyes, and predicted that this baby boy would reach the age of four-score and ten, would become a bishop, and would achieve wonderful things for God and the Church!

The strangest part of all this is, not that the prophecies came true (which they did) but that these two, Father Jerome (the Jesuit priest) and Alfonso Maria de Liguori (the future Redemptorist bishop) were both canonized, one hundred and fifty years later, on the very same day.

But, at the moment we are concerned with only one of these: St. Alphonsus. If you want to visualize him in his last years, as he rolled his wheelchair into the sunset, you should picture a man of medium build, clad in the black cassock of his order, olive-skinned in complexion, Roman of nose, peering through wire-framed spectacles, and wearing an aristocratic gray beard. With his head bent low by arthritis his chin had actually worn a sore on his chest.

By birth he belonged to the Neapolitan nobility, and as a precocious youth had entered the university to study law. Every biographer smiles at the scene where one day Alphonsus flounders up the auditorium aisle in an academic robe, much too ample for his young form, to accept a doctorate in canon and civil law. He was not quite seventeen. In the next eight years the youthful barrister never lost a case. Then came the day (one author suggests he was disgusted with the corruption and collusion around him) when Alphonsus walked out of the courtroom forever. He marched over to his favorite church, Our Lady of Ransom, and there hung up at her shrine his handsome dress-sword with its silver sheath and its clusters of precious stones. To us cold Westerners it all reeks of the theatrical but should it not be judged against its proper background — the act of a warm Latin, in a Renaissance country, in a previous century? Dramatically impulsive or not, Alphonsus was hanging up not merely his sword, but also his right to inherited wealth, his claim to a noble title, his prospects for a successful career — all these he left behind him, when he walked out of that church and strode away to give himself entirely to the service of God.

In his heart Alphonsus was anything but an aristocrat. It was not hard, then, for him to turn from the perfumed pack of young nobles with their velvet doublets and swirling capes and feathered bonnets. He never looked down a patrician nose on the poor as a ragged, smelly rabble. He saw in them the children of God. He made it the first sentence in the constitutions of the religious "order" that he founded that his men should labor for the most abandoned souls. In the beginning, these were the goatherds in the green hills above Naples, but eventually it had to include the unfortunates in the swarming slums of gray city streets. Today about eight thousand of these sons of St. Alphonsus, the Redemptorists, have spread across five continents, where like the Apostles of Pentecost, they preach the Gospel in a dozen different languages.

What Alphonsus accomplished in one man's lifetime makes you shake your heard in utter disbelief. As a composer, the young Alphonsus turned out many hymns that still ring out in Italian churches, including "Tu scende dalle stelle," the most popular Christmas carol in all Italy. As a preacher, Alphonsus conducted so many missions in parish churches, that when you follow his trail from pulpit to pulpit, you marvel that he found time to do anything else. As a bishop, although a reluctant one, he did for his diocese with its three hundred priests, what the Curé d'Ars did for his parish: made it a model Christian community. Incidentally, Alphonsus set the pace for all this by selling his golden pectoral cross and his ring and giving the proceeds to the poor.

Beyond all else Alphonsus was known as a scholar and an author. Would you believe that he turned out more than one hundred books? Most, of course, were slender volumes. Many were standard-size books. A few ponderous tomes bristling with the scholastic apparatus of learned footnotes. One researcher on Alphonsiana has estimated that his works in the aggregate have gone into more than a thousand editions and have been translated into more than fifty tongues. Not a bad monument for a man who was so devoted to work that he took a vow never to lose a single moment of time. Think of it; a vow not to waste one single moment!

The scratch of his busy quill still echoes around us. Drop into your parish church and lift your eyes to the golden door of the tabernacle. Do you know that the most popular prayerbook in honor of the Blessed Sacra-

ment over the entire world is St. Alphonsus' "Visits for
Every Day of the Month"? Look around you at the Stations of the Cross on the quiet walls. The most widely
used booklet in Europe and America for the Way of the
Cross has come down to us from St. Alphonsus. Remember how, when Lent was Lent, on Friday nights the
parish priest intoned, "No, Jesus, it was not Pilate. It
was my sins that condemned you to die . . ." Pure St.
Alphonsus.

Or slip into one of the confessionals, and the priest
behind the screen has long ago read all that you may
whisper, in the pages of St. Alphonsus. What Gray is to
Anatomy, and Blackstone to Law, Alphonsus is to Moral
Theology. Is it any wonder that in 1950 Pope Pius XII officially proclaimed him the Patron of Confessors?

Today we do not realize his impact on the world of
conscience, but had he not courageously opposed the
rigorism of his times, a Catholic Puritanism would have
hung its gray cloud over all the joyousness of Faith. Jan-
senism had woven around the communion rail a barbed-
wire fence of stern severity. The ordinary man was afraid
to approach the sacraments. Then came St. Alphonsus
with his keen mind and his distinctions, sharp as a wire-
clipper, to cut away all those fear-laden, false principles,
to open a path for the ordinary Christian to receive Communion.

It was for this, and for all his other solid contributions to Catholic thought, that the Church, over one
hundred years ago, accorded St. Alphonsus admission
into one of the world's most exclusive clubs. This circle
is so select that it makes the vaunted French Academy
look like a parcel of upstarts. We mean that small,
blessed and brilliant band of men (and now there are
two women: St. Teresa of Avila and St. Catherine of
Siena) whom we honor as Doctors (that is, Teachers) of
the Church. So seldom is someone tapped for this elite
group that nominations average about two a century. In
other words, in almost twenty centuries of Church history, there are less than forty Doctors.

St. Alphonsus' talents and achievements go marching through history. We see him as the young nobleman, as musician and composer, as successful lawyer, as learned theologian, as a holy bishop, as canonized saint, as Doctor of the Church, and finally as founder of the religious order we call the Redemptorists. Then ponder this. Alphonsus died as a man deliberately excluded from the very order he had established.

It broke his heart. To secure royal approbation for the order, two fellow Redemptorists who were acting as intermediaries for the aged and ailing Alphonsus, played him false, kow-towed to the king, and agreed to lop off a few of the order's monasteries. One was the very place where St. Alphonsus lived, and in which he eventually was to die. When the Pope, whose approbation had to be obtained, heard the true story, he exclaimed, "Good God! I have been persecuting a saint!"

By then St. Alphonsus had gone on to God. He died on an iron cot in the simple room of the obscure monastery of Nocera, not too far from Naples. Watchers round his deathbed were convinced he was gazing rapturously into the shining face of his beloved Madonna. Certainly his writings in defense of the Immaculate Conception in the eighteenth century strongly influenced the definition of that doctrine in the nineteenth. All his life he had been warmly devoted to the Mother of God.

When Alphonsus unhooked his handsome nobleman's sword and hung it as a votive-offering at Mary's Neapolitan shrine, he replaced it with the fifteen decade rosary that hangs at the side of every Redemptorist. Whenever Alphonsus signed his name, he added Our Lady's. . . . Alfonso Maria de Liguori. When he lay on his deathbed, his moist, feeble fingers clutched in their stubborn grip a paper picture of the Madonna. When the Fathers around his bed began the litany, his lips moved to join them, but no sound came forth. "Virgin most pure, pray for him! Queen of angels, welcome him!" And then, as if he were going up the golden stairs of the litany, he suddenly turned his head, smiled and died.

The calendar read August 1, 1787. And this is his feast day today, his birthday in heaven. To the sophisticated and yawning world it means little, but to Redemptorists on five continents it is Father's Day. Our Father who is in heaven!

Advent: Waiting for the Sunrise

If you know the background, you appreciate the achievement more. A man glances up idly at a super-jet streaking across the sky with its long white trail, like a silver fish running away with the angler's line, and he takes for granted that up there passengers are flipping through magazines or sipping cocktails or quietly chatting. To appreciate the marvel of that pressured cabin, hurtling through space at five hundred miles an hour, you have to remember Wilbur Wright's first egg crate wobbling above the Carolina beach for all of fifty-nine triumphant seconds.

In the same way, in order to appreciate the marvel of Bethlehem and the Son of God in the manger, you have to see it against the background of mankind's soiled and stained past. We cannot measure the height of the love of God that first Christmas unless we remember the depth of man's depravity. We speak sometimes in a picturesque way of God making man out of the slime of the earth. Perhaps we ought to wonder more often why He did not wash His hands of man and forget him.

Sin began with the beginning of man. This is a mystery of iniquity, that the very first human beings should rebel even in their garden of Paradise. But rebel they

did, and perverse humanity went on to become so bad
that sin crusted the world like soot, and God finally
opened the foaming heavens as a deluge to wash a dirty
world clean. You might think that this would be lesson
enough, but not for the malicious man. He went back to
his sin, like a dog to a buried bone, and this time his sin
grew so foul that it became moral gangrene. This time
water was not enough, so God sent upon Sodom and
Gomorrah the element of fire to cauterize the world's
poisoned wound.

You might think *that* would be enough, but not for
stubborn, stupid, sinful man. Now whole cities rose up,
dedicated to sin, like Babylon; cities where you could
not find ten just men, like Nineveh; cities whose streets
were highways to hell, like Corinth. After that, anointed
kings forsook God and went over to sin, like David and
Solomon. Then whole kingdoms abandoned the true
God and bowed down before the golden calf of idolatry.
Now, when God looked down from heaven to man, what
did He see? In his passions man was a lump of lust; in
his loyalty, fickle as a feather swayed by every wind of
temptation. All in all, he was an ingrate, practicing
through the centuries to be Judas.

Why did not God then walk away from man and forget him forever? This is precisely the marvel and the
mystery of Christmas, that all the million infidelities of
man could not swerve God from fidelity to His promise,
namely that one day He would send man a Redeemer, a
Savior for those who sincerely wished to be saved. The
wonder of Christmas is the way the Savior came, a baby,
with a thin cry in the cold blue air of a cave, and tiny
hands reaching out for love. One day that Child would
walk upon the waves and still the storm and raise the
dead and open the eyes of men born blind, but now His
own little eyes are hardly open.

This is what we celebrate each Christmas. Each Advent we stand on the eager tip-toe of expectancy looking
toward the radiance of a new star, to notes of a new an-
gelic song, to the birth of a new Child. Down the silver

steps of the bright evening sky, angels come trooping like children down a stairway to see their Christmas presents, and there in the stable they saw God's Christmas present to the world. It was so precious it was packed in excelsior, only the excelsior was the scraggy straw of a manger, and the present was a baby boy who was God's own Son.

There is the core of Christmas, and during Advent days it would be a pathetic mistake if the trimmings and trappings of the season made us forget the reason for it all — the crib. One little handful of the straw of Bethlehem, if we could hold it, would tell us more about Christmas than all the flamboyant ads that sing so lyrically of a hundred luxurious gifts. Any anticipation of the great day not built around the great fact of the coming of a Savior is hollow and empty.

It is like the incident of the young girl who lived in a furnished room in New York, fifty years ago. She had no relatives there, and no real friends. She was alone "in the heart of a city that had no heart." She was lonely but she was proud. So, a few days before Christmas, during her lunch hour, she bought some cardboard boxes of different shapes and sizes, some gift wrapping-paper and some gold twine. Then she stuffed the boxes with old newspapers, gift-wrapped them, and mailed them to herself. On Christmas Eve the postman blew his whistle, as they did in those days, and she opened her door. As the postman poured the parcels into her arms she could hear the faint creaking of other doors in the corridor, and she could sense the peeking of envious eyes, as the other boarders saw all these bright wonderful gifts. Then she closed her door, let the boxes drop on the floor and cried her eyes out.

In another and deeper sense, our Christmas will be just as hollow, if we make it consist only of the material things, the greetings, the decorations, the presents, and the rest. These are only the frame of Christmas, not the picture; only the vase, not the bouquet; only the ring, not the diamond. Amid all the lights and the excitement, the rush and the crush, we have to remember that the heart of Christmas is spiritual, or should be. It is joy over the coming of Christ.

For some of us, in that respect, the grandest gift-box of all could be the confessional box, where the guilt of sin is snapped as easily as the gay ribbons on a Christmas package. Like a Christmas cave, the confessional is a small chamber, but it still is where men of good will can find peace, and where straying sheep can find the Lamb of God.

If Christmas is essentially Christ, it is also Mary, for it is impossible to think of the Child without the Mother. We do not find it hard to picture her, mounted on the little gray donkey stolidly plodding the Bethlehem Road. That journey from Nazareth to Bethlehem was ninety miles, and usually took about four days. Joseph walked at her side, at once her guide and her guard. When you think of it, he was protecting the most valuable cargo this old earth ever saw. No Western stagecoach, no modern armored-car ever carried a treasure half so precious as the unborn Christ.

If you look at the picture from another angle, Mary with the Child under her heart, was like a priest going on a sick call, the Blessed Sacrament under his coat, his hand devoutly on his breast. Our Lady, too, was bringing our Lord to a sick world. Those would be cured who came near Him, even if they but touched the hem of His garment or the tassle of His cloak.

But our Lord came with His redemption for all time, and this is true of the intercession of Mary. His salvation continues through each new generation of men, and so does Mary's sweet but strong influence with her Son. In Bethlehem she knelt beside the rough manger with its bed of bristling straw and its hard, bleak poverty, but the same Mary is on her knees now before His throne of blinding glory and infinite riches. With a mother's warmhearted eloquence she can plead for any petition we place in her unselfish hands. If we are in tune with the true spirit of Advent, we shall ask her such gifts as a little more fervor in prayer, a little more kindness toward our fellowman, a little more gratitude to God for the gift of His saving Son.

He was so close to her heart, those first pre-Christmas days. May He be close to our thoughts now! Then we can be sure that for us, Christmas will dawn as the birthday of the long-awaited Redeemer, and not be just the holiday of December twenty-fifth!

Christmas: In the Center Is a Child

As Our Lady looks down upon this poor spinning earth she must smile a little at the shrieking contrast between her original Christmas and our current observance. Then, there was only a frosty road and a pair of quiet pilgrims, Joseph and herself, plodding the bleak route to Bethlehem. Now it is thousands upon thousands of chattering shoppers darting in and out along colorful avenues. Then it was a harsh, "No room at the inn!" and a great oaken door slammed in two pleading faces. Now at Midnight Mass in many a parish church there is hardly room for all the thronging guests of God. Then it was a handful of shepherds racing down from the dark hills in search of the Lamb of God. Now it is spiritual sheep, some of them black sheep and some oxford gray, returning to the fold at the Christmas call of the Good Shepherd. Then it was one gleaming star rising like a golden plume over a forlorn stable. Now it is a blaze of candles twinkling around uncounted altars. Then it was one single hidden cave. Now it is regiments of chapels and churches and basilicas and cathedrals lifting lofty and majestic spires to the sky.

In other words it is easy for modern Christians to fall into the spirit of Christmas. That spirit trembles and sparkles and hums all around us. It was not so easy for

Mary nor Joseph. For them no hanging holly, no glittering festoons of lights, nothing at all. They simply
trudged on, these quiet two, over a back road that
crawled away out of a second-rate village, Bethlehem.
They sought shelter in its lonely outskirts. In the inn
there was the rattle of dishes, the happy buzz of conver-
sation, the clashing of goblets lifted in unsteady toasts,
the roaring out of merry songs. In the city of Jerusalem
there was Herod, stroking his beard and plotting how to
rid himself of this mysterious young King that the Wise
Men talked about. In Rome and Athens and all the
world beyond there was the usual laughing and loving,
buying and selling, gambling and swindling, fighting
and dying, with nobody at all thinking of a midnight
cave at Bethlehem. You might just as well expect people
to be thinking that particular night of some Arab's tent
on the lonely desert or some hermit's hut on the highest
alp.   1897901
     That first Christmas the world was much too busy
to be bothered. Our Lord was literally left out in the
cold, the bitter cold of the stable-cave.
     Think how poor this couple was when they had to
share their shelter with a donkey and an ox! That was
the first Christmas Eve, with the darkness deepening,
the chill air numbing, the animals stamping restlessly.
Joseph whispered comfort and courage to Mary — how
far all this from a jolly, happy holiday! Was it not rather
a towering, trusting act of faith?
     In a way our problem is the opposite of the first Holy
Night. We have too much Christmas and too little
Christ. The emphasis is so much on the holiday and so
little on the holy day, or on the Holy Night. Consider the
Christmas cards. They glow with prancing reindeer and
steaming plum pudding, with red sleighs, red chimneys,
red Santas. Not too often do they frame a Bethlehem
crib or an Infant Christ. Leaf through an album of
Christmas cards in a department store, and the so-called
"religious" cards are but one small section. But is not
this what Christmas is all about? Christmas without

Christ makes about as much sense as an ice cube without ice.

Or consider the stores. At Christmas they become bright bazaars and commercial carnivals. The cash-registers play Jingle Bells and the thought of Silent Night would bring panic. Granted that all this buying and giving is a glorious gesture from generally selfish human nature, yet how many give truly in the spirit of the season? When they talk of the Christmas spirit, do they mean His spirit? When they give gifts, do they do it in honor of His birthday? And if not, might it not as well be Halloween or Labor Day?

In the miles and miles of crinkly, colored, holiday wrappings, how seldom do you see a hint of the Prince of Peace! In store windows how often you see Santa Claus and how rarely a straw-filled manger! So, our test at Christmas is just the opposite of Our Lady's. In the stable, before the Babe of Bethlehem came, Mary had to make herself believe, because everything was so cold and dark and lonely. With us, now that He has come, we have to make ourselves realize that He did come.

Everything around us is noisy, distracting, and leaping through neon signs. It has nothing to do with Him at all.

Not, mind you, that the Church wishes to dim the lights of Christmas. She does not want to take away one bright color, one silver song, one hearty greeting, one ribboned wreath, one happy surprise. It was the Puritans who wanted to turn Christmas into something somber and gray. All that the Church asks is that we do not lose sight of the tiny Christ against all the glittering background of the celebration. By all means, call out the merry greetings, sing the lilting carols, give the colorful gifts, enjoy the happy feast, but never forget we do it in His honor, in His name, for His birthday. The centerpiece of Christmas must always be Christ.

When the average man says Saturday, he never thinks of Saturn, after whom it was named. Saturn was only a god of Roman fiction and means absolutely nothing to a man of today. But when a Christian says Christmas, he should think of Christ, because Christmas recalls the day when God came down from heaven and became a man like ourselves, to live among us and eventually to die for us. *There* we have the reason, the only valid reason, why on Christmas our faces should shine like an illuminated tree, and our happy voices ring like sleighbells: for joy that God has come into our world, and that He lies there as our little Brother in the Christmas Crib!

Read the ads, and you come to believe that Christmas means many things to many people. But read the Bible and you find it should mean not things at all, but rather a person, one Person. The things should be only salutes in His honor, a salvo at the anniversary of His coming. What a pity, what folly if the Person whose day we celebrate gets forgotten in the very celebration!

You can never miss the meaning of Christmas if you raise your eyes to that celebrated Madonna, the Mother of Perpetual Help. That picture may be encased in all kinds of shrines, marble, golden, mosaic, or even simple wood. No matter what the setting, the picture itself always stands out like a huge bright Christmas card. In Our Lady's gown and in the Child's tunic it has the brave red and green of Christmas colors. Its background is the dusty gold of stable straw. On Mary's veil gleams a brilliant star like that of Bethlehem, and on either side angels float like the choirs of the Holy Night. In the center is the heart and soul of Christmas, the Child, safe and snug in the warm cradle of His Mother's arms.

That picture "tells it like it was." It reminds us that to keep a good Christmas we do not, for example, need snow; after all, half the world never sees snow at Christmas. What we do need is to welcome Christ. Without Him any Christmas is as empty as the hole in a holly wreath. At Christmas the modern pagan cries, "Eat, drink and be merry, for tomorrow we die." But the Christian toast is, "Eat, drink and be merry, for today Christ is born!"

Epiphany: A Word from the Wise Men

So many usually smart people make such flamboyant fools of themselves at New Year's that the Church, in a gently chiding mood, follows it quickly with the feast of the Wise Men. Till recently that date was January sixth, but since this is normally a weekday, and since the Church wants her children to hear the wondrous story every year, she has transferred the feast to the nearest Sunday.

That, of course, would never have been necessary in the Middle Ages. In those days people trooped to church on many a weekday, because that particular weekday was not only a holyday but also a holiday. Society at that time was rural rather than urban, agrarian rather than industrial, feudal rather than democratic. The Church then felt that one of the means of getting a fair deal for the non-unionized serfs was to increase the number of feastdays. Some historians maintain that in many parts of Europe the calendar was so checkered with holydays that there were more holidays than working days. It was the later Protestant ethic that canonized industry and diligence and thrift. The Catholic attitude was much more casual and happy-go-lucky.

At any rate, when the Fathers of the Church speak of the Wise Men, they emphasize not so much their learning as their wisdom. Granted, there is a type of man whose head contains so much information that his ears might as well be book-ends. Granted, his memory is a bric-a-brac cabinet of a thousand odd items. Granted, he could tell you (and if he gets the chance, he will) that the average depth of the canals in Venice is four feet; that a ventriloquist cannot pronounce the letter p, so that *please* comes out *glease,* only we do not notice it; and (to go from Venice and ventriloquist to Verdi) that whenever Verdi was asked what he considered his greatest work, he would always reply: "My greatest work is the retirement home I have built for old opera stars."

In that fragment of information, by the way, there are overtones of true wisdom. It shows that Verdi knew his scales, especially his scales of values, and that he put men above music, as humanity must always be above art. The weakest, scrawniest baby in the poorest hut in India is of higher value than the most magnificent masterpiece in the Louvre. That is why in a fire the firefighters would rescue a baby and let a painting (or an opera score) burn.

So the feast of the Wise Men reminds us that wisdom is not an accumulation of fancy facts but an appreciation of important truths. For example, it is the mark of a wise man at the beginning of each New Year *to make sure* that his sights are set on serving God and meriting heaven. As time goes on, the best of us stumble. Our high resolves slip, and, like violin strings, need tuning. At times the fire of faith itself burns low.

Recently I was in a very old office building. A grayhaired lady sat behind a typewriter, her fingers tapdancing over the keys. Occasionally she stopped and blew on her hands. "It gets pretty chilly in here," she said. She reached out and touched an ancient radiator. "This is a 1900 heating system, and this radiator is actually the last one on the line. By the time the heat gets to us it has lost all its enthusiasm."

I suppose it is somewhat the same with our resolutions. They start off flaming with fervor at New Year, but as the year wears on, the spirit wears off. By bleak December the fire has all but gone out, and that is why we have to stoke the blaze as the New Year begins. They say the good die young, and this is particularly true of good resolutions. With this reservation: these can be revived.

New Year comes in January, which curiously calls to mind Rio de Janeiro, the River of January. Our whole life is like a river. It rises in the clear bubbling spring of childhood, broadens into the great sweeping stream of maturity, and finally flows into the vast ocean of eternity. It is in that middle stage, when the river flows through the city of worldly experience, that it so easily becomes soiled and polluted with garbage and scum.

One way of purifying water is through chlorination. And there is a way, too, of purifying the polluted soul. We call it confession, meaning that genuine sorrow on our part will elicit generous pardon on God's. In these post-Vatican II days, confessional slides scrape open and shut less frequently than they did even a few years ago. It would not be a bad New Year resolution to seek sacramental absolution each bright new calendar month.

We should toss into the waste basket our old way of life, together with the old calendar. There should be an end to all the old, devious, conniving compromises, and in their place initiate a complete spiritual turn-about. The change will resemble one of those rare rivers with reversible falls. In such a stream the water comes pouring downward at ten in the morning in a fuming, frothing roar. At four in the afternoon the same water goes rushing upward in swirling, angry foam. It is an infrequent phenomenon and requires extraordinary conditions.

In the same way, for a man to reverse the whole course of his moral or spiritual life is a rare achievement, and requires a very special grace from God. It is something beyond nature, and requires the supernatural. Ever since original sin, you and I, as children of a fallen race, are constantly tilted toward evil, forever pushed on by passion, always tending downward by a kind of moral force of gravity. It is not our nature to stay good constantly. It is no more natural for a rock to burst into bloom, for a fire to shoot up into a fountain, than for an ordinary human being to walk for long on the path of goodness without falling. Even St. Paul moaned that he did not always do what he willed to do, but, alas he often did what he hoped he would not.

To combat this, Paul (or any of us) needs the supernatural help of God. Try, if you want, to see without eyes or to breathe without lungs, but do not even try to keep the Commandments without the special assistance of God.

Many a man has smugly thought, "I can read that daring book. It won't throw its pictures on the screen of my mind and influence my thoughts." Many a heavy drinker has said, "I'll go out with the boys and take one drink or two. I'll stay in complete control." Many a young pair have conned themselves into imagining, "We'll go parking again, but this time we'll just talk." This makes about as much sense as saying, "I'll put my finger into this bottle of ink, but I'll make sure it doesn't get stained."

What is all this except smug, foolish futile pride? The only rebuttal is: down on our knees, and up with our prayers! The New Year resolution we all need make is to beg heaven for help. Not every three months, but every morning when we rise, every evening when we retire, and in between whenever temptation rings our doorbell!

To whom shall we turn? The Wise Men "found the Child with Mary, His Mother." In heaven they are still together, and the wise men and women of today still find them there through prayer. Our Savior has all the power. His Mother has the sweet influence that sways Him. Because she was so close to Him at the crib in Bethlehem, so close to Him in the cottage at Nazareth, so close to Him at the cross on Calvary, she is closest of all to His throne in heaven. From the Wise Men she accepted gifts. With us she is eager to give gifts, especially the gift that the wise Christian seeks — the sincere will to serve God.

Lent: It Was Never Really Repealed

Ash Wednesday means that the gray curtain is going up on another Lent. On that bleak stage the only plot of this oldest of all morality plays is the cemetery plot, the usual reminder that death, which is always happening to everybody else, will eventually happen to us. "Ask not for whom the bell tolls, it tolls for thee," wrote the poet John Donne.

Donne wrote another line which I cannot remember verbatim, but which comes to mind each Ash Wednesday as the people pour out of church wearing badges of gray dust smudged on their solemn foreheads. He noted how the wind blows the dust from the churchyard cemetery in through the open church doors, and then later the sexton sweeps the church dust back into the churchyard, so that no one can tell which is the dust of the living and which is the dust of the dead. Does not Shakespeare hint somewhere that the speck of dust in your eye may be Julius Caesar?

If one half of the lenten stage portrays the inevitability of death, the other half proclaims the iron necessity of penance. There is need here for a clean and drastic distinction. The old Lent with its endless paragraphs of legalism, has been modified to a mildness that would have shocked our grandparents. But notice that the

Church has not abolished the need for doing penance. She did not and she cannot. What Christ Himself has commanded not even the Church can countermand. And when He commands penance, the usually gentle voice of the Savior grows strangely stern and the text drops like the blade of a guillotine: "Unless you repent, you shall all likewise perish."

Then, to show that He meant more than interior sorrow, Christ launched into the parable of the fig tree that was cut down because it did not bear fruit. *Works* of penance are the fruits of repentance.

In this tradition our mild modern Lent does not make penance obsolete; it only makes it voluntary. From now on the ideal lenten program proceeds not out of the lengthy regulations drearily droned from the pulpit, but from the choice of the individual Christian. The ashes of Ash Wednesday are to come from a heart of fire. Penance is no longer allocated; it is a la carte.

This would be fine except that all around us, like an invisible deadly fall-out, there drifts the damnable propaganda that penance is passé, medieval, out of style and out of date. The truth is that penance will be out of date only when sin is out of date. Does anyone really believe that when the last oxcart went creaking over some obscure American road into the horizon of history, that sin was seated alongside the driver? Is it not the sad truth that today, when our roads are paved, and cars purr across them, there is as much and maybe more sin than before? Never mind the century; whenever sin batters down the majestic statue of God's commandment, it is not enough that contrition murmurs, "I'm sorry." Penance must get down on its knees and humbly pick up the pieces.

The same world will also try to tell you that penance is cruel, almost barbaric. In that case Christ was the great barbarian, because it is He who enjoins and endorses penance. The fact is that the very things the Church suggests in the way of penance millions of people are doing all the time, except that they do them for another motive. It is one more case of doing the right things for the wrong reason.

Take the matter of fasting. For the holy cause of fashion or in the sacred name of diet, people will starve themselves with the wistful hope of streamlining down from a shapeless snowman to a slender icicle. They do it for the lard's sake, but they won't do it for the Lord's sake. Or take the matter of whittling off three quarters of an hour's sleep once or twice during the week to attend Holy Mass. How many young people carve two or three hours off their sleep (admittedly from the other end, the heel of the night) for pleasure! They will do it for dancing. They will not do it for the Deity.

Or take great-grandfather's Lenten practice of parking his pipe on the mantel on Shrove Tuesday night and leaving it there till Holy Saturday noon. Nowadays more and more crisp young executives are throwing away their last pack of cigarettes because they have heard the fearful whisper of lung cancer. Overnight they give up tobacco forever for fear of cancer, but they would not do it for six weeks for love of Christ.

When a doctor hints at the danger of diabetes, people do not find it hard to bypass candy and desserts. When a stomach ulcer begins to twist its hot iron fist in a man's innards, it is not too difficult to lay off firewater. When a girl sets as her goal a stylish figure, it suddenly seems reasonable to wave away cream puffs and measure out calories like a miser. But, when the calendar quietly announces Lent, these very people have three dozen excuses. Is the reason perhaps because we love ourselves too much and God not enough — or not at all?

There is really only one valid argument that can be adduced against lenten penance, and that is that it is hard; that it hurts. But do we throw into the river everything unpleasant and distasteful? If we have an infected finger, we are willing to submit to the surgeon's scalpel. If we have a bad tooth, to save it we are willing to endure the dentist's drill. If we must get to work in the morning, we are willing to obey the icy burr of the alarm clock that routs us so rudely from a warm and cozy bed. How many things in life are hard — and necessary? Put lenten penance in that class. Certainly it is not pleasant, and just as certainly it is indispensable. It is penance or perish.

Why is penance so necessary? In one of the most somber texts in all Scripture St. Paul darkly intimates that every mortal sin is another crucifixion of Jesus Christ. If in a man's life he had only one black Good Friday afternoon when, through mortal sin, he crucified Christ, would a dozen Lents be enough to atone? But what if his soul is a mountain range of Calvaries, every hill dotted with a cross of serious sin? Should he not be even glad of Lent's reminder and opportunity for penance?

When temptation urges to slacken self-imposed lenten penance, let us lift our eyes to a crucifix and think what His last Lent was like. Take a good long look at the thorns stabbing into His head, at the agony glazing His eyes, at the thirst baking His swollen lips, at the mud and blood smeared on His face, at the twisted torture of His sagging body, the last fearful choking gasps for breath that finally stifled Him. Can we look at this and not be willing to suffer a little for the Lord who suffered so much?

Keep the mitigated lenten laws of the Church, of course. Beyond that, decide on something more. Make it definite, make it generous, and make it stick. Do it gladly, not grudgingly. Then it will not be long till the ashy cinderpath of Lent leads us to where glorious lilies trumpet their silent joy over the empty tomb of Easter!

Easter: Risen — As He Said

One of the first things a young priest learns about Easter in the practical ministry is that a sermon has to be short. On that day the time is needed for the real sermon, which does not ring from the pulpit but files silently from the pews as the people march up to the Communion station in the best of all Easter parades.

More than once our Blessed Lord had predicted His resurrection. "The Son of Man will go up to Jerusalem and be scourged and spat upon and crucified, and on the third day He will rise." Although there was no such thing in those days as a coroner's death certificate, a death could hardly have been better established than was the death of Jesus Christ. When a victim had suffered the tortures of crucifixion for some hours it was customary for an executioner to batter and shatter the victim's legs with an iron bar. This induced shock and hastened death. At Calvary the soldiers did this to the two thieves. They did not do it to Jesus because their practiced eye told them He was already dead.

But the centurion was taking no chances. He, after all, was responsible. To be doubly sure, he wheeled his horse to the cross and drove his lance into Christ's side. A little blood and water poured out, like an epitaph.

Then Joseph of Arimathea, who was a wealthy Jew

and who had some influence with the Romans, went to Pilate and asked permission to bury the body, for he had secretly believed that Christ was the Messiah. Pilate would not hear of this till he received official notice of Christ's death. So the centurion presumably investigated once more and sent word back to Pilate. Only then were the Holy Women allowed to take the body and prepare it for burial. When they laid it in the tomb that Friday afternoon they certainly had no doubts that Christ was dead, because when they returned after the Sabbath they brought the spices customarily used for burial.

But forget about the soldiers, the centurion, Pilate, the Holy Women, and merely remember that Jesus was surrounded on the cross by the snarling group that had called out for His blood, the mob led by the Pharisees and the Priests. Would they have been satisfied with anything less than death for this Christ? In fact they were so certain that He was dead that they asked Pilate for a guard around the tomb, so that the body could not be stolen. "Because this man had said that on the third day he would rise."

Did He rise? History and logic come forward together to testify. If Christ did not rise, then the Apostles were either fools or they were frauds. They were either gullible and taken in, or they were sharp and promoting a racket. Were they gullible and naive? As a matter of fact, they themselves were so far from being eager to believe in the resurrection that when the Holy Women came back from the tomb with the news that it was empty and that Christ had risen, "to their minds the story was madness" (Luke 24:10).

Such men would never be content with any second-hand evidence. And they did not have to be. Later Christ came to them, *the doors being shut,* and they saw Him with their own eyes. They saw Him not just then but many times thereafter. They saw Him not at a distance but close-up. They saw Him not in a flash, like a magician's trick, but over a space of six weeks, the period before He ascended into heaven. They saw Him when there was not just one witness or two or three, when you might suspect hallucinations, but with a dozen others, then a score, once two hundred, and once five hundred.

The Apostles not only saw the Risen Christ. They heard Him. They ate with Him. They touched Him. When Thomas heard that the others had seen Him, He shrugged. "Believe what you like," he said, "but as for me, first I want to put this finger into the nail-holes in His hands, and this fist into the spear-wound in His side." Soon after, when Thomas was with the other Apostles, to his embarrassment he was invited by Jesus to do just that.

As to the Apostles being frauds, what would be the motive? Money? But the first Christians were poor and shared their goods in common, like holy and dedicated communists. Fame? When they preached Christianity the Apostles were laughed at in learned Greece, persecuted in outraged Jerusalem, and forced underground in Rome. What did they get out of it? Peter got prison, Paul got chains. John got boiling oil.

They all eventually got the violent death of martyrdom, except St. John who was saved only by a miracle. Frauds do not die for their causes. They make a rich living out of them. And, as Pascal reminds us, we more easily believe that a man is telling the truth when he is willing to have his throat cut as witness to his testimony. The Twelve did just that, all but Judas who hung himself on Good Friday morning and so never did see Christ rise.

And make no mistake about this. The Resurrection is the core of Christianity. How else could a dozen fishermen (think of twelve longshoremen today) with no money, no education, no languages, no prestige, no influence, launch the Gospel? How could they take on at once the establishment of the Jewish religion and the power of the Roman Empire?

They could not appeal to patriotism. Christianity

went beyond national borders. They could not appeal to pride. Christianity preached humility. They could not appeal to the passions. Christianity preached purity. It offered man nothing for which his fallen nature craved and it commanded him to give up so much to which his pagan appetites had clung. And yet within one-hundred and fifty years the Christian faith reached almost all over the known civilized world. Surely behind it there had to be the power of God! God endorses only the truth, and what these Apostles preached as the very central doctrine of the faith was the resurrection of Jesus Christ.

If Christ had not risen, He would have been buried under the words falling like clods on a coffin, "suffered under Pontius Pilate, died and was buried." Christianity would have been only a musty curio in the museum of history, a two-inch footnote in an encyclopedia. But if, instead, Christianity proceeded peacefully to topple over the towers of great empires, to form the very framework of our civilization, to give culture the best of art and music, and even to become the schoolmaster of man's conscience as nothing else ever had been, it was only because the founder of Christianity rose from the grave.

This is what we celebrate at Easter. Otherwise, "It might as well be spring." But spring is only drowsy nature stirring and stretching after a long winter sleep. Easter is Christ flinging away His shroud and bursting from the tomb. Easter should be for many of us the flinging away of another shroud, the winding-sheet of some tyrannical sin, and the bursting out of the tomb of some imprisoning passion. After Easter some will go back to the old evil. This is like a man morally climbing back into his coffin. To rise and to stay risen requires more than Easter Communion. It demands frequent Communion. May those who at Easter have found their way after a long absence from the altar follow that path every single Sunday! They will find it leads at last to Christ, glorious in heaven, who will welcome us, not merely to a Happy Easter but to a happy eternity!

Ascension: Under a Cloud

In this neck of the woods (New England) it has been a rainy Spring, but now the good Lord, who has been walking down the long green aisle of the land scattering His holy water in the liberal showers of an April Asperges, has at last laid down the sprinkler. Soon, we know, He will lift the great golden monstrance of the sun and swing it over us in bright and shining weather. Midway, however, between sun and rain hangs the lingering cloud, and with May comes the feast of the cloud, the Ascension of our Lord Jesus Christ into heaven.

When our Savior reached the end of the Mass of His life, He turned to give the final blessing to the Apostles. They bowed to receive it and then saw to their astonishment that they were looking only at His footprints. Christ Himself was slowly, majestically ascending into heaven. As they looked up, a cloud covered Him and He was lost to their straining eyes. Is there not some vivid symbolism in that strange detail, namely that Christ should leave us "under a cloud"?

How many good men have lived and died and gone to God under a cloud! Most of us, at some time or other in our lives, have been under a cloud at least for a little while. Perhaps you are a woman, and some close friend has told you a secret. and then suddenly the secret is out and you are accused of betrayal. How can you prove that you did not reveal it? How can you ever prove a negative? You are under a cloud. Or maybe you are a man and the grimy insinuation gets around that you are dishonest in your business dealings. How do you prove that you are innocent? The more irresponsible the mud that is flung, the more it seems to stick. Because of it, you go to your daily work under a cloud. Or, and this is worst of all, the person in all the world that you love best and truly and only, begins to voice suspicions that your affections have wandered, or even to charge you coldly and bitterly with unfaithfulness. There is not a thimbleful of truth in all the baseless suspicions, but you feel within you a broken heart, and under your own roof you live under a cloud!

This is the time to remember that our Savior in a sense left this earth under a cloud, but the next moment was seated on the sparkling throne at the right hand of His eternal Father. It might also help to recall that more than one shining saint plodded and stumbled and groaned along under a cloud till he found his glorious vindication. How many know that St. Patrick, after he had worked for more than twenty-five years planting the faith in pagan Ireland, facing every kind of danger, enduring every sort of hardship, was turned upon by his best friend, reported to Rome and deposed from his office? Patrick's first reaction was black despair. Then he tightened his lips, and travelling through Ireland under that cloud, went off to Rome to clear his name. He was reinstated, of course, but oh that long dark tunnel of abandonment and lonely disgrace!

It must have been a dark day in the life St. Alphonsus Liguori when some spiteful woman came to him with a black-hearted and venomous tale about Brother Gerard Majella. She was sure he had acted immorally with a certain young girl. She flung the charge in the young brother's teeth. St. Alphonsus demanded that the girl herself be brought to confirm it. But the girl, he was told, had since moved off to a distant part of the country.

St. Alphonsus drilled the woman with his gaze, then
turned to St. Gerard. "All you have to do is to tell the
truth and declare your innocence." St. Gerard only
stood there and said nothing. The Redemptorist Rule, he
knew, forbids a religious to defend himself. Well, the ordinary Redemptorist would interpret this in the sense
that if for example he had carelessly left his window
open when he went out, and a storm came up and the
rain sloshed over his desk and the superior saw it and
reprimanded him, he should in such an instance humbly
and silently accept the reprimand. It certainly does not
intend to enjoin silence when a man's moral character is
attacked. But young Brother Gerard was a saint, and
sometimes saints see their religious rule as a straight
car-track to be straightly followed and not as a fork in
the road with a free-wheeling choice. So when Gerard
was accused, he could not be persuaded to say anything
in his defense. He would say absolutely nothing.

The trouble was that nobody could see the inside of
Brother Gerard's mind and almost everybody presumed
that silence gave consent. Even St. Alphonsus felt he
had to forbid Gerard to receive Holy Communion, and
was in fact taking steps to strip him of his religious garb,
when suddenly the long arm of God reached down and
touched the accuser with a grave illness. When the slan-
dering woman was convinced she was about to die, she
blurted out to the people around her bed that she had
wronged the young Brother out of spite and that her
whole story was a malicious lie. Granted the tale thus
has a happy ending, but what about the days when
Gerard lived among his brethren like a leper, under suspicion, under a cloud?

If St. Gerard Majella was almost run out of his religious order, there were other saints who knocked in vain
at the doors of certain orders that they yearned to enter.
St. Joseph Cupertino, St. Camillus de Lellis, St. Benedict Labre were all dismissed at one time in their lives as
being impossible material. Don't you think each of them
dragged himself away from that monastery door de-

spondent, under a cloud, and yet (such is the irony of God) each of them eventually marched through the gates of heaven as a canonized saint.

The list of saints who lived at least for a while under a cloud is practically a litany. How many people, who see the superb Don Bosco Trade Schools that meet a major need so magnificently in so many major cities, are aware that their founder St. Don John Bosco, was all but railroaded into an insane asylum as completely demented? St. John of the Cross (to cite a similar case) was left to languish for weeks in a Spanish jail under the charge of violating some grave point of Church law.

But the old sayings are true. "The mills óf God grind slowly but they grind exceedingly fine." The cloud eventually lifts. The elders stone the prophet and then their repentant sons gather the stones and build a monument to the martyr. Or, as in the case of St. Joan of Arc, who was burned at the stake at Rouen and possibly Savonarola who was hanged and burned in the square of Florence and whose canonization has been proposed, how fitting the poet's vindication in verse:
"The hooting mob of yesterday in silent awe return/ And gather the scattered ashes into History's golden urn."

It must always happen this way for one simple reason. God has time. He does not close His books at the end of a year. He keeps them open until right triumphs and justice prevails. When a good man dies under a cloud, he goes like Christ from a brief shadow to the eternal radiance of heaven. So if you are being misjudged at this very moment, blamed for something of which you are utterly innocent, walking under the cloud of undeserved suspicion, the Ascension is your feast. Lift up your heart and realize that God's keen eye pierces the cloud and sees your guiltless heart.

There is one cloud that inevitably overshadows us all, and that is bereavement. Here too the Ascension is our comfort. Did it ever occur to you that the Ascension is stronger, in its way, than any other feast in the calendar? Do we not on this day celebrate Christ leaving us,

yet the Mass rings with the music of joy? We lay aside in
other words our own loss, our own loneliness, and rejoice
at the happiness of another. We exult that His suffering
is over, and He is now secure and serene in the realm of
heaven. Should not this be our attitude too, after the
first understandable shock, when we lose a dear one who
has gone to God? We should not spend too much selfish
time in pitying our own loss but instead turn prayerful
thoughts to our loved one's gain and glory.

Even Our Lady knew what it was to live under a
cloud. When she was mysteriously pregnant and could
not reveal the miracle, and when a perplexed Joseph
struggled in his soul and all but decided to send her
away, an angel revealed to him that Mary was still a virgin and was to be indeed the Virgin Mother of God. In
the meanwhile, Mary must have winced under his in-
quiring gaze and felt a blush flaming in her cheeks. For her
the happy ending came when the Lord of the Ascension,
finding even paradise lonesome without a Mother, drew her
up to Him in an Assumption of her own, where Mary (as all
the painters conceive it) floated heavenward not under a
cloud but enthroned in one and trailing it like a robe of
glory.

Sacred Heart: The Crimson Flame

Before his conversion, the late Monsignor Ronald Knox had been an Anglican. More than that, he was the son of an Anglican bishop. He was therefore superbly equipped by birth and background, plus a brilliant and richly-stored brain, to mingle with his non-Catholic friends as a kind of one-man ecumenical movement. When one of these asked him about "this business of devotion to the Sacred Heart," he smilingly countered by asking a question himself. "Now who do you suppose was the author of the book with a two-story title called, *The Heart of Christ in Heaven Toward Sinners on Earth or the Tender Affection of Christ as Man Toward Mankind in its Misery and Sin?*" Whereupon the lean monsignor chuckled inside his oversize Roman collar (it looped his neck as loosely as a ship's life-saver around a broomstick), and pointed out that the devout author was a Congregationalist minister named Thomas Goodwin, and of such good standing that he had attended Oliver Cromwell in his last illness, and had even closed those celebrated eyes in death; a luxury, he might have added, that many an Irishman might have envied. The good monsignor was only gently trying to make the point that this Puritan book, with its old-fashioned title rumbling along like a row of freight cars, really sums up Catholic devotion to the Sacred Heart as capably as could any cardinal.

Some non-Catholics might be soured toward our cult of the Sacred Heart because of the images of the Sacred Heart they see in religious article stores. For that matter, many Catholic churches, presumably because they can afford no better, have pictures of the Sacred Heart that are run of the mill, or statues that are run of the mold, and that portray such a banal, bland, confectionery Christ that it might make a Catholic like Michelangelo faintly ill. In his play *Shadow and Substance,* Paul V. Carroll has a scene where the two Irish curates have just hung such a picture of the Sacred Heart in the rectory, when the elegant monsignor (Irish, too, but educated in Spain) sweeps into the living room, bores the picture with appalled eyes, and waspishly comments, "If I believed for one moment that our divine Savior ever looked like that atrocious chromo, I would forthwith give up my faith." Precisely what *did* our Lord look like? It is not easy, in painting or in sculpture, to come upon everyone's ideal of God made man.

Besides, in the usual picture or statue of the Sacred Heart there is the unusual feature of the heart being openly displayed. Incidentally, that heart alone may never be portrayed for public devotion. Liturgy demands that it always be represented as reposing in a human figure. Even so, the curious non-Catholic will ask, why this emphasis on the heart? What does it signify? And is all this something recent or does it have roots sunk deep in tradition?

Here we must make a distinction. From the time the earliest Christian reader pondered the New Testament page where the Roman centurion plunges his lance into the side of Christ, he must have thought of the Sacred Heart. What else was the target of the spear in that intended *coup de grace*? To that extent at least, attention was focused on the Sacred Heart from the dawn of Christianity. But, just as there were radio waves long before there were radios, and atoms with locked-in power long before atomic submarines, it was a long time between the first Good Friday and the first Feast of the Sacred Heart.

Most beginnings are small. Even the Mississippi, monarch of our rivers, is at its start only a thin thread of silver slithering through a dark pine forest in Minnesota. In the same way the devotion to the Sacred Heart is only a faint crimson glimmer in the writings of St. John and St. Paul, but it grows brighter in the works of St. Bonaventure and St. Bernard, and bursts into the brilliance of aurora borealis in the pages of St. John Eudes and St. Margaret Mary Alacoque.

So much, briefly, for the development of the devotion. And its message? With all the devotional suet hacked off, the meat of the matter is this: we honor the Sacred Heart as the *symbol* of our Lord's love for mankind. After all, we live by symbol. We have the red lantern of danger, the blue ribbon of excellence, the white flag of surrender, the black ball of condemnation. It is true we do not need symbols in the sense that we could survive without them. For that matter, we do not *need* a flag flying over troops on parade; we do not *need* a riderless horse at a president's funeral; we do not *need* the Washington Monument. On the other hand we are not disembodied spirits; we are flesh and blood beings. We are creatures of sense, of sight, of hearing; and these material symbols do help to express our ideals and emotions, and do help to inspire our conduct.

The heart is the universal symbol of love. The Sacred Heart is the symbol of our Savior's love for men. That, by the way, is the reason why the sacred Heart is never portrayed with anatomical accuracy in picture or statue. Instead, it is a perfect or symmetrical heart, because the heart here does not represent a mere physical organ, but the seat of an emotion, the symbol of affection or love.

Furthermore, this particular symbol seems to have divine endorsement. It happened in the little town of Paray-le-Monial, which is about five hours by train from

Paris, in the region of France known as Burgundy. To many of course, Burgundy is famous for its sparkling red wine, but it deserves to be remembered much more as the place where the Sacred Heart, that crimson chalice of the Precious Blood, was revealed as a special object of our devotion. The year was 1673; the day was two days after Christmas, very appropriately the feast of St. John, who is represented in paintings of the Last Supper as resting his head on the heart of Christ.

In the wintry dusk a slender young nun knelt transfixed in prayer before the convent altar. She was only twenty-four, and had been in the cloister but three years, but she must have loved our blessed Lord wholeheartedly, with never a speck of her heart attached to any person or thing. Nothing in this world meant anything to her except in God or for God. So to her our divine Savior appeared in that quiet chapel, revealing His own Sacred Heart aflame like a red tabernacle lamp. "This is the heart that has loved men so much, and is so little loved in return."

Our Lord reappeared to her on many occasions. When she confided all this to her confessor, the saintly and scholarly Claude de la Columbiere, he felt she should inform the Mother Superior. Mother Superior, like many of her tribe, was a blunt and practical woman who decided that the best remedy and the strongest rebuttal for visions was less time spent in chapel and more time assigned to peeling potatoes, scrubbing floors, and (as a sure death-blow to all mystical experiences) tending the convent donkey. When the apparitions persisted, a committee of three learned clergy sat on the case and gravely recommended that "the little nun should eat more, especially more soup."

Eventually the long arm of God reached down to perform some startling wonders and thus establish the sister's veracity, sanity, and sanctity. She lived on for fifteen more years, never once leaving the convent grounds, never breathing her experiences to a soul beyond the cloister. It was Father Columbiere who relayed the revelations of the nun to the world outside.

Curiously, the message of our Savior to St. Margaret Mary was almost the opposite of the usual picture of Christ as the Sacred Heart, which tends to express sugary sweetness like an oversized valentine. But what our Lord showed the holy nun was not a joyous heart but a broken one, wounded by the sins of men and looking to holy souls for comfort. Any tourist to Paris knows the bohemian section called Montmartre with its crooked streets crawling up the hill in a blaze of gaudy lights, and a blare of nightclub noises, a shrill chain of dens and dives. Every pilgrim to Paris knows that at the top of that hill shines the luminous dome of the Basilica of the Sacred Heart, gleaming like a clean white pearl. Inside there is perpetual adoration. There you have in one single vista the story of the Sacred Heart: sin and atonement.

When our Lord appeared to St. Margaret Mary, He showed her His heart encircled with thorns. Why were the thorns around His heart and not around His head? A boy answered that question once, perhaps better than any theologian: "Maybe because our sins hurt Jesus more in His heart than in His head." Actually the Savior put it another way to St. Margaret Mary. He said: "Long ago my enemies struck me in the face, but my friends wound me in my heart."

It was no mere coincidence that our blessed Lord appeared to the saint precisely at the time when the Jansenists, a harsh band of Catholic heretics, were preaching doctrines that fell upon the faith in France like a numbing frost. Yes, they said, there is a God. But He is a God of justice and of no mercy. Yes, Christ died for men, but for only a select few. Yes, Holy Communion is the food of the soul, but unless you are perfect, do not dare approach the altar more than once a year.

It was to cut through this barbed wire fence of severity which the Jansenists were raising between an all-loving God and an all but despairing mankind, that Jesus Christ broke the silence of divinity and spoke to St. Margaret Mary. Certainly He was grieved by man's sins; surely He wanted saintly souls to make reparation; but His heart, opened once on the cross by a Roman spear, could never be closed to any sinner who sought refuge, pardon, and peace.

If Christ asks atonement, it is because His human Heart yearns for reconciliation. He is the Lord who loves to be loved. Many years ago somebody noticed that atonement was really at-one-ment. At-one-ment means union; in this case, Communion. The best way to atone for the past is to be at one with Him in the future through frequent and fervent Communions, a faint echo of those nine precious months when the heart of Mary beat in rhythmic measure with that Sacred Heart which loved her — and us — so much.

All Souls: Fingerstring Feast

We say of a proud man that he has a fat head. We say of
a sympathetic man that he has a soft heart. We say of a
forgetful man that he should have a string tied around
his finger.

The feast of Christmas strikes the proud man in the
head, right between the eyes, if he lets those eyes fall
upon the crib. There he sees the vast majesty of the Almighty cramped within the four little boards of a
manger. Who could be proud as he looks upon the infinite become an infant?

The feast (if we can call it that) of Good Friday
strikes not the sympathetic man but the Christian of
any sensitivity whatever in the heart, for the great wood-
en pulpit of the cross with its silent preacher thunders,
"Look! See what your sins have done! If you had not
gone to the tree of forbidden fruit and plundered it,
stripped it, there would never have had to be this gaunt,
bare tree of the cross, whose only fruit is the bitter fruit
of your guilt, the bruised, blood-running fruit of the
Body of God!"

November the Second is not the feast of the crib nor
of the cross but rather of the coffin, the feast of All Souls,
and this is the feast that gently tugs at the string around
our finger, quietly nudges our memory, pleadingly asks,
"Have you, too, forgotten?"

Poor, fickle human nature! Think of the last loved one you left in the cemetery. When that dear mother of ours died, or that good hard-working dad, or that husband or wife, brother or sister or darling child, we never dreamed we would forget them. Not for so much as one whole day. We would have blazed with anger if anyone suggested that weeks or even months might fly by and we would never remember them. Why, at that grave we were burying part of ourselves! The loss was like a string ripped from a violin; it could never make the same music again. It was like a precious stone tumbling out of a ring and leaving an empty, tell-tale space.

This is the way we thought, as we came away from the open grave and glanced back to see the flowers banked around in bright beauty. We knew that soon those flowers would wilt. Sooner than that even, a whistling wind might whirl them away, and eventually the cemetery people would have to clean up the untidy mess in the name of neatness. But we consoled ourselves that deep in our heart we had planted a forget-me-not that the soft tears of memory would keep fresh forever.

And that is the way we thought as our heavy steps brought us back home, the strangely empty house, bleak house. Here the very furniture all but cried out, and so many things reminded us of her. There was her favorite chair near the window, now so starkly vacant. There was her coat hanging in the closet, so limp and forlorn. There was her brooch lying on the dresser. It used to sparkle so brightly. Now it seemed to be blinking back the tears. A dozen things pleaded, "Remember!"

But memory is like a ship. When it is close up, it looms huge, tall-masted, towering. As it sails away, it grows smaller and smaller, till it becomes only a dot on the distant sea, and then dips over the horizon and out of sight. We take no notice anyway; we are too busy in the bustling harbor of everyday affairs.

That is precisely why the Church on one day of the year tolls its bell like a lighthouse, and bids us remember those who have drifted away on the purple tide of death.

It is an appropriate time of the year too — dull, gray November, when the last rose of summer has faded and died; when the leaves have fallen and the black branches of the trees look like the border on a memorial card; when the very sunsets seem subdued and the dull western streamers hang like ribbons of crepe over the doorway of the world.

Though the Church asks us to remember our dear departed, she does not want us to be morbid about it. I knew a police inspector in the Bronx who had seen dozens of dead bodies in his day, but when his own wife was buried he would not let them close the coffin. For a few wild moments he was not himself. No doubt it is one thing to drop a blanket over a unidentified corpse on a city street, or to look down into the ruffled white silk of a casket where that marble mask of death is only a casual acquaintance, but when the face there is a fond, loved face that swims before your eyes — this is something else again. Still, our grief should be under control. We should not "sorrow as those that have no hope."

Most of us who admired Hilaire Belloc this side of idolatry could not see his mourning glory. Belloc, with his square jaw and his squat solid figure was the living cartoon of John Bull. He was also, besides being a brilliant essayist, a lucid historian and a rollicking poet, the very pattern of the highly educated English Catholic. Yet, when his wife died, he turned the key in the door of her room, and never entered it again. Each night as he went to bed he would pause and make a sign of the cross upon the panel. For the thirty years he survived her, he wore only sober black. Even his letterpaper was edged with black.

Call it what you want: it was eccentric, excessive, extravagant. Most of us err in the other direction, insofar as we so seldom think of our dear departed or the possibility of their being in Purgatory. Purgatory? A word in the Catechism. Something sad and far off. Because it is sad, we sigh and shake our heads. Because it is far off, we shrug our shoulders and murmur, "What can *we* do?"

If the hands that reach pleadingly out of Purgatory to us are hands that we once clasped, Purgatory cannot be so far away. And we can help. Not by sending *Care* packages but by sending *prayer* packages. The very month of November is the Church's air-lift, bound for Purgatory and loaded with Masses and indulgences.

A couple of days after All Souls Day we keep the feast of St. Charles Borromeo. In the midst of a fearful plague this tall aristocratic cardinal cared for the sick and carried the bodies of the dead to the cemetery on his strong shoulders. Our devotion to the dead need not be that dedicated, but on our shoulders does rest the responsibility of ransoming those dear ones who may be in Purgatory. We do not fulfill this merely by keeping All Souls Day any more than we would keep Lent by observing only Ash Wednesday. What we ought to do on All Souls Day is to decide on something that we shall do for our departed on every day in November. Make it specific; make it generous; and make it stick.

Suggestion; a quiet little rosary takes less than ten minutes. And it can be the reason that the perpetual light will shine upon them. And upon us too, when our time comes, in reward for our Christian remembrance. Let that string around your finger be the twining little chain of the beads!

Thanksgiving: Some Thoughts About Thanks

If any day in the year is a switch, it is Thanksgiving. Just as it would be a switch for the man to bite the dog, or for fishes to fly high in the sky and birds to burrow deep under the earth, it is surely a change when we stop whining "gimme" to God and instead pause to thank Him. It used to be that in the average silver coin, like a dime or a half-dollar, the content was ninety percent silver and only ten percent alloy. But in our average prayers perhaps there is ninety percent asking and only ten percent acknowledging. Surely, though, there is enough to acknowledge! It is said that the key most often struck on the typewriter is the letter *e*. It is almost certain that the word most often hit by a man on his knees is *please*. A compilation of the ordinary man's prayers might turn out to be a hundred pages freckled with phrases like, "Deign, O Lord," or "Grant, dear God," or "Please, my Jesus," while the expressions of thanks could be relegated to a few footnotes.

Sometimes, it is true, we do express our gratitude. Sometimes when an angel, as it were, rings our doorbell and lays in our hands a very special favor, we actually give thanks. For how long? For about as long as it takes to sign for a special delivery letter. And from then on all our attention is on the gift, and the giver is forgotten.

But Thanksgiving is that extraordinary day in all the year when even the dullest is moved to thank God for all the evils He has spared us, and more especially for all the goods He has heaped high around us — if only we would open our narrow, selfish eyes to see them. In fact this is the day when the Mass itself can take on a fresh meaning, if we turn our attention, as we should, to the Preface. Just *before* the most sacred part of the Mass, just *before* Jesus becomes the food of our souls as He did for the Apostles on the first Holy Thursday, just *before* He offers His Precious Blood to His eternal Father as He did on the first Good Friday, just *before* this, the priest intones the ringing prayer which literally means "before." This is the Preface, a solemn hymn of thanks to God for all the gifts that have come cascading down to us up to that moment.

"Let us give thanks to the Lord our God!" urges the celebrant. "It is right to give Him thanks and praise," agrees the congregation. "Always and everywhere" the text emphasizes. And then, if it be a special season of the year, priest and Preface go on to thank God for some particular kindness.

Around Christmas the Preface thanks God for the star of Bethlehem, that first candle to twinkle on the altar of Christendom when the world was dark in paganism. During Lent the Preface sings its gratitude to God that when the tree of poor human nature was toppling to its doom in the garden of Eden, Christ came to prop it up with His cross. On the feast of the Sacred Heart the Preface thanks God that when the heart of our Savior was slashed open by a soldier's spear, it became thereby a hiding place and a refuge for sinners. Even at a funeral the Preface sends out its prayer of thanks over the body of the deceased, rejoicing that for this faithful child of the Church, life has not been taken away but only changed to a better one. Never a Mass is said but its Preface is a burst of gratitude. The very chalice of the Mass is not a beggar's cup held out trembling and pleading for an alms, but a golden goblet lifted high in a toast of thanks to our tremendous benefactor, God Almighty.

When we were little children it was natural that we looked upon our parents as a kind of supply depot for all our wants. Mother and father were the grown-ups who provided us with a bed to sleep in, a house to live in, perhaps a yard to play in. When it was time for dinner we took it for granted that dinner would be on the table. When Easter came, we knew we would get some bright new clothes. At Christmas or on our birthday there were special presents like toys. We never wondered where these fine things came from; we just were sure they would be there.

When we grew to man's estate, we began to look back at our parents in a different light. We no longer looked upon them as the people from whom we got something; instead we realized how good they were to give us all these things. Our attitude changed from a child's instinctive grabitude to an adult's appreciative gratitude.

Should it not be the same in our relation to our Father in heaven? When we are in the spiritual kindergarten our prayers are bound to be only *please, please, gimme, gimme.* As we mature in character as well as in age, then more and more in the orchestra of our prayers the clear trumpet of thanks should blare its solo. If it does not, are we not playing the thoughtless, selfish child?

At the family dinner table when we pass a dish to a youngster and he does not say, "Thank you," we reprimand him. It is simply courtesy to acknowledge something by saying "thanks." What then does our Father, God, think of *us* if all day long and every day of our lives we are snapping from His hands the gifts He gives us — like life and health and friends and faith — and we hardly nod in His direction! The French have a piercing proverb, "Gratitude is the memory of the heart." Have we no heart?

Surely we do not have to be reminded what we should thank God for. Each has his own reasons. Let the cook thank God for her roasts, the doctor for his cures, the bookkeeper for his balances, the farmer for his crops, the priest and the nun for their vocations, parents for their children, and children for their mothers and fathers, and all of us for the Church and the sacraments and the heaven to come! If every single tree in the grove of life's blessings has been planted by one master gardener, then we who enjoy the fruit and share the shade should daily give thanks to that gardener, who is God!

Someone once had the horrible idea that we should reverse the whole idea of Thanksgiving. Instead of dedicating one day to thanking God, this cynic proposed that we set aside one day for complaining and murmuring and grumbling and griping to our hearts' content, but then on all the other days of the year we should give thanks. Perhaps he had a point. Perhaps he was not a cynic but a saint.

Every Thanksgiving I find myself thinking of a superb priest who died in his forties. When I knew him he had an exceptionally agile mind and a pathetically helpless body. He had led his class each year in the seminary, and then served for twenty years in the same parish. Everybody loved him. He was the spiritual heartbeat of the neighborhood. Then one day he collapsed at a funeral Mass. The attack was diagnosed as the same strange paralysis that felled Lou Gehrig of baseball fame. After that it was heartbreaking to see him inch across the room hunched over his two canes. And yet his spirit soared up on eagle wings. If one picture is worth a thousand words (but notice, incidentally, that the man who launched that idea used words to do it), then one visit to this sunny invalid was worth a thousand sermons.

What I remember most was how many of his sentences ended with "Thank God." And "Thank God" came from him as naturally as water leaping from a fountain. When I would gently sympathize with him, he would smilingly brush it aside. I remember once he said, "You make too big a deal of my setup. Being sick isn't the worst thing in the world. When you are well, there are all kinds of activities to make you forget God. But when you are sick, you simply can't forget Him. You remember Him, you pray to Him, you get close to Him."

And, in a little while, out from between the grim parenthesis of those two canes would come another "Thank God."

He would be a strange man who on Thanksgiving Day can stand up and look around and not find anything for which to thank God. At least he could thank Him for the feet to stand on and the eyes to look around.

OUR LADY

Mary, Her Place and Her Power

If you told a convict who was swinging at the prison rockpile that Shakespeare had said there were sermons in stones, he might think you had rocks in your head. Yet to some geologists, rocks have been stepping-stones to faith. Such men have come striding over these boulders toward God as if they were the front steps of a church. They have gone from the study of the ages of rock to the discovery of the Rock of Ages.

Though every rock is a kind of silent monument to God (for it did not make itself), the most you can say of the average rock is that it exists. If we go to the next plateau of creation, we encounter life and growth, as in the flowers of spring that lift their tiny gay parasols above the meadow, or the summer trees that hold their great green banners like a parade that has just come to a halt. Then, comes a new, higher level of life — the world of sound and motion, the world of the oriole's golden flight and bubbling song, the world of the panther's smoothly poured leap and savage snarl.

At the very peak of the pyramid of this globe's creation stands man — man with his vocal speech and his written literature, his music and his art, his science and his government, his mind and his soul. The smallest man can stand before the tallest mountain and scorn it, because he can measure the mountain's height, photograph its shape, catalogue its minerals, fly over its summits and even (with a few nuclear bombs) remove it.

If mankind stands at the top of the spiral of creation, there is one human being who stands in the forefront of mankind. This is Mary, the maid of Nazareth. When Jesus did what no mere man could ever do — choose his own Mother — and chose Mary, He automatically made her queen of humanity. For the next nine months, her immaculate body became more precious than any jeweled chalice in the world ever could be. For the following thirty years, she was sacristan and priest to guard and serve the humble tabernacle of His Nazareth home.

The bond between Jesus and Mary went beyond the physical fact that hers was the womb that bore Him and hers the breasts that gave Him milk. Did not Jesus Himself later point out that there was something much higher than this? "Yea, rather blessed are those that hear *the word of God* and keep it." Mary had heard that word at the Annunciation. The angel offered her the towering responsibility of being the Mother of the Messiah. With bowed head she answered, "Be it done to me according to *Thy Word.*"

From that moment those two hearts would beat not merely in the delicate intimacy of Mother and Child, but in the deeper spiritual union of the divine Lord and perfect subject. Unlike the rest of us, Mary, full of grace, never wavered for a single instant in doing the will of God. If her body gave to the Savior His human flesh, her soul gave Him unswerving adoration and unfaltering allegiance. Her life was one shining sea of goodness. She died in the end like a flower that finally droops on its stem at the altar, having served its God to the last. Mary was the mystic rose.

She was also the morning star, as the litany hails her too. As the morning star hangs above the horizon, apparently close to earth yet unsmirched by its smog or grime, so Mary walked this world untouched and unspotted by any of its sin. At the first flash of the sun's dazzling rim, the morning star quietly recedes. And, so too, when Jesus, the glorious sun of redemption first began to shine forth His public life, Mary humbly retired into the background. After all these ages, the morning star is still there, crisp and bright; and after all these centuries Mary is still there, too, the symbol of purity, the guide by which we can steer for heaven.

Mary is more than a guide toward heaven. She is an influential intercessor with the Lord of heaven. On one occasion, a little group of Greeks sought an audience with Jesus. They decided to approach Philip first, because Philip lived in the seaport town of Bethsaida where the natives were bi-lingual in Hebrew and Greek. Philip brought the delegation to his fellow townsman, Andrew, because he felt that Andrew had been with Christ longer and knew Him better. It ended with both Philip and Andrew escorting the band of Gentiles to Jesus.

By the same logic should not Mary have more influence with Jesus than anyone else? Did she not know Him longest? Was she not closer to Him in every way — closer to Him in the cave at Bethlehem, closer on the hill of Calvary, and closer today at His throne in heaven?

If they are so close, would not Jesus find it hard to refuse His Mother? If Noah prayed and God promised that no future flood would ever wipe out the human race; if Josue prayed and the golden wheel of the sun seemed to stand still so that daylight would hold and the battle might be won; if Moses prayed and the Lord hurled the horrible series of plagues at the homes of the Egyptians; if Samuel prayed and the rains came drumming on the dry earth, drenching the soil and saving the harvest — how much more persuasive must be the prayers of Mary, who is in rank higher than all these, in merit richer, and who holds gentle and affectionate sway over the Lord who rules everything!

No wonder the saints have dared to call Mary, "omnipotent on bended knee." They mean by this that her

prayer is so irresistible that when she kneels down to ask
— God bends down to answer.

We are so happily blessed in having Mary as our intercessor in the bright court of heaven. We should realize
that this situation is no one-way street. If we have the
right to call upon her as our Mother, do we not have the
obligation to behave as her children? In the art galleries
of the world, we can see many concepts of Mary the
Madonna depicted by the masters. To some she was
light-complexioned and golden-haired. To others she
was, like the Mother of Perpetual Help, olive-skinned
and dark-eyed. To them all the Child in her arms had to
be a miniature of the Mother. In Mary's case this was
especially true because there was no natural father. The
Child must have been the perfect image of His Mother.

We are Mary's spiritual children. We were born, not
as Jesus was, without pain or pang in the stable of Bethlehem, but in anguish and agony on the bloody mount of
Calvary when Jesus said, "Woman, there is your son!"
In that immortal moment John stood for us all. Since
John's own mother (Mary of Klopa) was there beneath
the cross, there can be no doubt that Jesus spoke of a
spiritual motherhood. But if we are all her spiritual children, should we not resemble our Mother, not in feature
or face, but in conduct and character?

One day, I was walking along a busy avenue toward
the hospital and heard a lad of about nine shout to his
pal on the opposite sidewalk, "I can't. My mother
doesn't want . . ." A truck rumbled past and I never got
the last words. I knew what he said, and the thought
came that for anyone who really loved his spiritual
Mother, Mary, there could not be a better motto to hang
over the door of temptation, than the boy's terse
clincher: "I can't. My mother doesn't want me to." Be it
a dance or a date, a book or a show, a pleasure-outing or
a business deal, anything smeared with dirt, the answer
should always be: "I can't. My Mother doesn't want me
to."

Then one day when we stand before the gate of

heaven, timid and trembling, that Mother will recognize us, not by our looks but by our life, and say, "Son (daughter) behold your Mother! Won't you come in?" Not for just a few minutes, but for all eternity!

Visitation: Minor Feast, Major Lesson

In the mountain range of Mary's feasts there rises the snow-capped summit of her Immaculate Conception and the towering peak of her Assumption into heaven. Admittedly, among feasts like these, the Visitation must be reckoned down in the foothills. But there are those who love it and cherish its lessons. Besides, it commemorates a visit that is still vividly remembered, while many other visits, on the surface much more important, are quite forgotten.

In the Spring of 1939, one visit made screaming headlines. At that time Hitler was flexing his military muscles, and England and the United States were getting nervous. To bind the English-speaking world closer together, the King and Queen of England paid an official visit to New York City.

What an occasion it was! Overhead, wedges of planes roared past in thunderous greeting. In the harbor, a battleship boomed out a flaming salute of twenty-one guns. Along the avenues were hundreds of thousands of people strung out like miles of dark wire — wire that was charged with electric excitement, wire that, as the royal limousine purred by, crackled with applause and flashed with bright flags. A royal visit, a royal welcome, a glittering reception, a stupendous ovation! Who ever recalls it today? What does it mean to us now?

That is where the feast of the Visitation is different. Nineteen hundred years ago another Queen and her little unborn King took part in a visit that was ever so simple. He was Jesus Christ, the King of Kings, and the Queen was Mary, the Lily Maid of Israel, His Mother. She had heard that her cousin Elizabeth was with child and needed help, so up from Nazareth Mary journeyed, along the winding brown roads, between the rising green slopes, up into the hill country, as the Gospel calls it. Perhaps the flowers waved their tiny flags as she passed. Perhaps the tall cedars stood at stiff attention like an honor guard of grenadiers. Perhaps, but very unlikely. What we can say with certainty about the Visitation is that nineteen centuries later it is still happily remembered by many and still has its impact on the lives of men.

Consider for a moment the case of nuns. It is sadly true that in these years of turmoil in the Church we hear of nuns departing the convent for careers. We cannot exactly call them the faithful departed, because that would be perhaps only half right. Furthermore, we should judge no man, or no woman. Let us not forget, however, that the nuns who have closed the convent door behind them are only a minor fraction of the sisters who have stayed. To these the Visitation means much, because on this feast all across the Catholic world in thousands of convents the sisters renew their vows, their lifelong consecration to the service of God.

Or turn to the ordinary priest, whether he be Jesuit or Redemptorist, Dominican or Diocesan. Each day as he recites his office from the priest's prayerbook, the breviary, he repeats the words that Mary spoke on that visit, the Canticle of the *Magnificat:* "My soul magnifies the Lord and my spirit rejoices in God, my savior." So after all these hundreds of years the feast of the Visitation still touches the prayer-life of the devout priest every single day.

Or look at the laity. Look at it this way. There are on this earth about four hundred million Catholics. That means that each day millions of "Hail Marys" float up to the throne of God like a great fragrant incense-cloud of prayer. Where did the Hail Mary start? The heart of it is from the greeting of Elizabeth to Mary, when Our Lady visited her: "Blessed art thou among women, and blessed is the fruit of thy womb!" In that sense, the Visitation of long ago echoes and re-echoes in morning prayers and night prayers and rosaries in our own day.

The most astonishing angle of this rustic visit has to be Mary's response. In what tone did she speak it? Certainly not boastfully, not arrogantly, not presumptuously. Her words must have been soft and calm, and trembling with a kind of unbelieving awe, as she said, "All generations shall call me blessed." It had to be said humbly because was ever a prediction so brash? Here she was, an unknown girl standing in an obscure mountain cottage, in a forgotten village, in a conquered country, the daughter of a despised race, and she quietly prophesies that in all the centuries to come she will be called blessed.

God must have been speaking through her lips. How truly it has all come to pass! Grope through the shadowy catacombs of ancient Rome, and you will find frescoes on those rough walls depicting the Virgin Mary. Stand in the square of a medieval town and you will see its majestic cathedral, like Chartres, soaring up in dizzy spires and gorgeous glass to honor the Virgin Mary. Slip into any Catholic church in our nuclear age and you will find a picture or a statue of the Virgin Mary, and often before it a vigil-light stand with rising tiers whose flames flutter like tiny pennants waving in a grandstand, a joyful salute to that Queen whose visit is still remembered when other queens lie long forgotten in their dusty tombs.

Has the Visitation any practical message for our modern life? The same incisive lesson it brought to the early Christians and the Middle Ages! All we have done is change the jargon. The emphasis today is on making religion both vertical and horizontal. The vertical thrust is our aspiring prayer to God. The horizontal sweep is the broad stretch of charity reaching out toward our neighbor. Does not the scene of the Visitation enclose both in its golden frame? Prayer we have there in the original Hail Mary. And practice, too, in the fact that though Mary's heart was turned to God, her hands were stretched out to help her neighbor, in this case Elizabeth.

That is why Mary visited Elizabeth — to bake the bread, to make the beds, to spin the flax, to sweep the floor, to tend the fire, to do what should be done for a neighbor in need.

How different, to go far afield, is Mary, the humble peasant, from Dostoevski, the groping intellectual. Dostoevski professed to love humanity but confessed he could not stand human beings. Mary loved God and, as we know from the Visitation and the marriage feast of Cana, loved her neighbor for the love of God. May 31, feast of the Visitation, reminds us as Christians that we can never be independent of any neighbor in need. We are more than our brother's keeper. We are our brother's brother — or sister. If he is poor, we must do what we can to assist him; if he is sick we should visit him; if he has been bereaved, we try to console him. This is the visit of Mary taken out of the Gospel and transferred to the ghetto. It is sanctity on the sidewalk. In a way it is graciously returning Mary's visit of long ago.

Say It with Flowers

Each year the American nation dedicates a day to its mothers, and each year the Catholic Church in America dedicates a whole month to the Mother of God. Flowery May is the chosen time. " 'Tis the month of our Mother, the blessed and beautiful days." "To the fairest of Queens, be the fairest of seasons, sweet May!" In our latitudes, at least, May is a charming season. Even in the inner city, where the only trees are iron utility poles, and the leaves are candy wrappers skittering along the scarred sidewalk, and the sunsets are neon signs blazing in front of bars — even here at least the air of May blows soft and gentle.

In the rural areas we find the real May, a scene so attractive it might have been something that drifted out of heaven when some cherub forgot to close the door. Overhead, nature flings forth a sweep of serene blue sky with puffs of white clouds that might be water lilies floating on a lake. On the ground, nature unrolls its richest carpet of tender green strewn with gay flowers as if for the bridal march of a young princess. In the verdant woods the trees are near full leaf and often touch fingertips together so that when you walk beneath them it is like the lofty arch of a dim cathedral aisle. In the apple orchard the dark tree trunks and the snowy apple blossoms form a procession of priests in black cassock and white surplice, while the choir of golden-throated birds sing, and the very air is perfumed like a sanctuary at benediction. Little wonder that the Church likes to look on the lovely landscape of May as a giant floral offering laid by God at the feet of His Mother.

Still, there may be ecclesiastical changes afoot. The old song asked, "Will you love me in December as you did in May?" It is a question we may have to ask of ourselves in reference to Our Lady. Now the movement is only a ripple on the devotional sea, but such things can become rolling swells. There are those who would change Mary's month to December and they argue that in many parts of the world May is an ugly month, raw and wet and chill, a scene of rain and mud. Besides the relation between Mary and May is just an indirect connection, poetically founded on mere nature, while the relation between Mary and Christ is direct and close and permanent. Mary is nothing without Christ, as a sunset would be non-existent without the sun. December is the month when Mary was heavy-laden and when she brought forth her Child to become the Mother of God. Let December then, they say, be Mary's month, and let it fit snugly into the Advent cycle, and let us in spirit walk by her side each December day along the Bethlehem Road, until she brings forth the little King. Sentimentally and traditionally I still like the month of May, but logically and theologically December has its points. Perhaps what essentially matters is not devotions in May, but devotion to Mary.

However, May at this moment is still Mary's month. That does not mean that in honoring Our Lady the poetical should blind us to the practical. Life is not so much a garden as a truck-garden, with its work and dirt and worms and sweat and produce and disappointments. We don't live at the foot of a Maytime shrine but in a grimy world. As Catholics we look to Mary as our national patroness, but she certainly is not the universally acclaimed heroine of America. You do not see her picture in public places, her statue in any park. The heroines of the hour, if you can judge by prominence or notoriety, are not the Queen of Heaven or the Queen of May but the faces that simper from theatre billboards, enameled faces of a sultry and sinister beauty, like flowers in a swamp that lure a man on and then drag him down. It is tragic to realize that such brazen creatures actually do have an impact on people's lives, and win imitators and create trends.

We who strive for saner and more wholesome goals can look beyond these to Mary, the model of pure and gracious womanly goodness. If we do, her very memory will help us, man or woman, to be good. She will help us quietly, because she needs no flamboyant fanfare of publicity nor a press-agent's wordy build-up. Who was it that first noticed that the silent moon, by shining in its dazzling whiteness, draws all the surging waters of the globe to itself? So Mary's purity will draw our murky and troubled souls toward herself, if we but let ourselves come under her influence!

Certainly we shall do this if we love her. Love and May both say it with flowers. But our love must be a living flower, not wasted and dead. There is always danger that when we pray to Mary, especially in a weekly novena, we pray mechanically, routinely, as if our love were nothing but a dried-up petal in the pages of a prayerbook. This is wrong. Mary is human, we are human: between us there should be a pure affection that is like a fresh, dewdrenched flower lifting its inspired head even in the soot and grit of our prosaic daily life.

Say it with flowers . . . not with buds. A bud is like a tightly closed little fist, holding on to everything it has. There are people like that, selfish and ingrown, who are interested only in themselves. What a contrast to a full blown flower, its petals all expanded, and its rich fragrance flung generously in every direction! Yet God sees to it that such a rose still has plenty for itself. If we call Mary our Mother of Perpetual Help, should we not, as her children, give at least temporary help to anyone?

Say it with flowers, but not with the flowers that flourish only under the sheltering glass of the greenhouse. That is like the pallid virtue that flourishes only inside the stained-glass window of a church. A sturdy flower has to thrive in the world of biting frost and blistering heat, a world of hailstones that pelt down and of gales that tear up. So our practical virtue, our imitation of Mary, has to stand up in a world of dates and dances, business deals and insurance policies, novels and plays, family troubles, studies, disappointments. Anybody can be good in church. True love of Mary survives its tests in the real world.

In other words, say it with flowers, but mostly with fruit. In our rectory backyard we have a tree which during May soars up as a superb spectacle. The pale delicate cones of its blossoms point up like a huge Christmas tree trimmed with white candles. It is by far the handsomest tree about, but in a short time it changes into the messiest, amid a welter of useless horsechestnuts. It is the perfect picture of the man with fine, polished manners, but with scurvy morals. Not by their frills, but by their fruits you shall know them!

Some of us, looking back on our lives, may think that we have never really loved Our Lady; we have never said it with the flowers of true love or the fruit of good deeds, but spiritually and morally our lives have been an ordinary pile of dried hay or worthless yellow straw. To such the cry comes rolling down from heaven, "Courage! Be of good heart!"

Was it not on the old yellow straw of Bethlehem that Our Lady laid the new-born Christ? So, on the straw of what we may think was a futile and wasted life, Mary can still set the new-born Christ. New-born, because May is the month of beginnings. Sorrow for the past is a groan for a grim winter gone by. Resolution for the future is springtime in the soul. The best is yet to be!

Help of Christians

The Litany of Our Lady is a sparkling necklace of brilliant titles, each stone standing for some particular Marian glory. There is one particular gem that flashes back the dramatic fire of history in the gleam of swords and chalices. It is the invocation, "Help of Christians, pray for us!" Pius V incorporated this into the litany after the Christians' miraculous victory over the Turks at Lepanto.

Three centuries later, another event raised that title to a feastday of its own in the calendar followed in Rome. This story is less known. It was the drama of an emperor and a Pope, characters as widely different as any two people could be. The emperor was Napoleon Bonaparte, the one-time little corporal in the faded green uniform, later still favoring green but wearing the gold epaulettes of the world's highest general. The other was Pius VII, thirty years older and his hair turning white, and wearing the cream-colored cassock of the world's highest bishop as Pope of Rome.

Napoleon had waded in blood to a throne whose foundation stones were the tombstones of defeated enemies. Pius VII every morning took his devout stand before an altarstone and offered the Blood of Christ to God the Father. Napoleon conquered kingdoms and gave them away to his relatives. Pope Pius was zealous and jealous about only one kingdom, the Church of God.

Then came the confrontation. When Napoleon invaded Church lands, the Pope hurled at him the ultimate penalty, excommunication. From every public square in Rome the white document fluttered for all to read. Napoleon was not impressed. He only sneered and asked, "Will an excommunication make the muskets drop from the hands of my soldiers?" Then he sent troops pouring into the papal palace. They packed the saintly Pope into a carriage that soon was rattling across the French border.

After that coup, when Napoleon complacently surveyed the captured battle flags in his great trophy room, he could smile even more broadly. Now he had a new and very rare trophy, a captured Pope. Why not, the thought surely came to him, use this captured pontiff to negotiate a divorce? After all, divorce had long been in the emperor's thoughts. Since his wife, Josephine, was barren, Napoleon wanted to discard her and deal himself another queen. The Pope could put the papal seal and signature on the document, and make everything respectable in the eyes of a naive world.

If Napoleon had spent less time in making history and more time studying it, the temptation to use a Pope might never have come. He would have remembered how far King Henry VIII got with Pope Clement VII, when the answer came back, "Non possumus." As straight as that. "We cannot." Or Napoleon might have recalled his own experience when he tried to arrange a papal annulment for his younger brother, Jerome. Jerome had married an American girl named Patterson whom Napoleon did not approve. With the petition for annulment that Napoleon addressed to Pius VII, he thoughtfully sent a handsome new tiara which the goldsmiths of Paris had worked frantically to finish. But emperor's brother or no emperor's brother, tiara or no tiara, the same answer fell like a dull echo: "Non possumus." "We cannot."

Perhaps this was what had then prompted Napoleon to decide he would engineer the annulment of his own marriage himself. He would first lay the matter before the churchmen of the Chancery of Paris. He did this, and predictably they saw things in the emperor's light and granted him his decree. And of course the Pope would sign *that*. But old Pius VII, prisoner though he was, shook his white head and refused to recognize the mockery.

Now came Moscow when the muskets did fall from the frozen fingers of Napoleon's soldiers, and the bodies of so many brave men lay like logs in the snowdrifts, and the hail rattled its drumbeat on the drums of drummer-boys stretched stiff in death. This was the grand army of five hundred thousand who had marched into Russia behind Napoleon's proud eagles. Only about fifteen thousand came limping back, half-frozen fellows with beads of ice on their beards and eyebrows, and with rags bound round their tattered shoes.

Napoleon's portion of humble pie had been cut even larger than this. After the whistling snows of Moscow came the red rain of Waterloo, that battle of mud and blood and utter defeat. The last act was the bleak, lonely island of St. Helena where Napoleon lived out his final few years like an eagle chained to a rock, its wild eye sweeping the vast skies and its wings beating the ground in helpless fury.

Have you noticed, in all this, how everything that Napoleon did to the Pope, God seemed to do to Napoleon? In the castle of Fontainebleau, Napoleon had wanted the Pope to sign a marriage annulment; in that very castle, Napoleon had to sign his own abdication, giving up all claim to the throne. For five and a half years, Napoleon had held the Pope a prisoner; for five and a half years, Napoleon was a prisoner himself. Napoleon had carried the Pope off to exile in France; Napoleon was exiled to a gray little island in the south Atlantic. Napoleon had broken up lands of the Church like a chocolate bar and distributed them among his friends;

the Pope lived to see the empire of Napoleon split and splintered among the emperor's enemies. The mills of God grind slowly but they grind exceedingly fine.

In the meantime, Pius VII returned to Rome. He was jubilantly received, the head of Christendom come back to the heart of Christendom. He was no longer prisoner, but pontiff, no longer exile, but ruler. The day he entered the eternal city was the twenty-fourth of May, and he put that day on the calendar observed in Rome as the feast of Mary, Help of Christians. This was his way of saying thanks, because on each lonely, harassed day of his captivity, he had prayed to Our Lady for deliverance.

The French have a saying, "He who eats the Pope dies." A century later the hands of the great clock of history came around once more to the same moment, when another little corporal, another conqueror, came to Rome. Hitler rolled into the city in a shimmering black limousine, preceded by banners that flaunted the crooked, twisted cross of the swastika. Another Pope Pius, Pius XII, to show what he thought, left Rome when Hitler entered, and went off to Castel Gandolfo, some miles away. Hitler shrugged off the deliberate snub, and snarled that the whole structure of the Catholic Church was so rotten that one good blow would make it collapse.

Would it? The Church remembered the other little corporal, Napoleon. She remembered another emperor, Nero. She remembered barbarians like Attila the Hun who had tried to trample down the Church under the hooves of his savage cavalry. She remembers diplomats like Bismarck who wanted to legislate the Church out of existence in the name of culture and education. The Vatican art galleries were crowded with the statues and pictures of men who had been bent on wiping out the Church, but they were all dead, and the Church was vibrantly alive. The anvil had worn out the hammers. The Rock had stood, and the waves had broken into a froth of muttering failure.

The Church survived not because there had never

been weak rulers on its throne, nor wicked members in its ranks, but simply and solely because Christ was with it, in it, within it. And because Mary was the Mother of the Church, the Mother of Christians. If we invoke her under that same title, she will bring to us in our personal trials the same comfort and courage she brought to Pius VII, and end them, if it be God's will, with the same happy outcome.

They Don't Go to Church Anymore

People stop going to church for different reasons. Some grow indifferent and stop gradually, like the propeller of a plane slowly flipping over till it comes to a dead halt after the motor has been turned off. The solution to that situation is simple — switch the motor on again. To put it another way, the honest man looks into the mirror of his conscience and finds no sounder grounds for giving up God than laziness or inconvenience. He skips church not because he does not need it but because it requires an effort.

There is another type of man who does not passively stay away from church but deliberately boycotts it because somewhere along the line he had a quarrel with a priest. But refusing to darken the door of a church because of some unpleasant incident with an individual clergyman is about as logical as never eating ice cream because you were once snubbed by a milkman.

A third group is more pitiful. They are not lazy, and they are not bitter, but they are sensitive and timid and tend to have tissue-paper souls. Deep inside they want to come to church often, to draw closer to God, but they stay away because they fear ridicule. To be honest, they do not fear it; they have felt it. Over the rattle of the typewriters in the office, or against the clatter and tinkle of the cash register in the department store, or between deals at the bridge game — there are so many places where you can hear the smart sarcastic remarks that the world reserves for those it considers "too religious." By too religious it means anyone who is foolish enough to drop into church during the week, or anyone who lets the hearts-and-flowers world of religion clash and interfere with the bread-and-butter world of reality.

As long as you limit your religious program to being only a fashionable and musical way of spending Sunday morning (on those Sundays when you have no other engagement) the modern world is understandingly tolerant. Once you go over that quota, once you let the spirit of religion seep into your daily life, once you let the ideals of Christ and Christianity run like a golden thread through the ordinary homespun fabric of routine everyday affairs, once you let your standards stand up and condemn an inflated insurance claim, or an expanded expense account, or a crooked deal in business, or a scurrilous attack on the Church, or an appealing piece of political graft — prepare to be ridiculed. The snipers will get you and their shots can really hurt.

It is quite possible that there actually are men and women who, had they lived in the grim days of persecution might have suffered gallantly for their faith but in this soft and sneering time, when the persecution is ridicule, they wince and surrender. The one thing they cannot stand is ridicule. Today that may be the precise test; not being killed for your faith but being kidded. Not being surrounded by crackling flames but by cackling laughter. Not being tossed on the horns of a wild bull but being lifted ever so gently on a raised eyebrow. Is it possible that people have actually been taunted and laughed out of heaven and into hell?

Certainly the world has often tried it. Certainly the world has often tried to cram the dunce cap of the fool on the saints who wore an invisible halo. As a matter of fact, even beyond considerations of religion, almost everything on this old globe that ever grew into something

worthwhile has at some time or other been fertilized
with ridicule. Read the story of almost every great man
and you find that the first notes of his trumpet of
triumph were the braying laugh of some insulting
jackass. Did they not brand the first steamboat "Ful-
ton's Folly?" Did they not mock the suffragettes who
only asked for what now everybody takes for granted —
the right of women to go to the ballot-box and vote?

In the area of religion, there were probably those
who winked and smirked when Washington knelt in the
snow at Valley Forge. Surely there were those who hoot-
ed St. Francis out of his home town of Assisi. Of course,
the ordinary man does not think of himself against such
a dramatic background. He knows he is not an heroic figure, the photograph in the frontespiece of a book. He
only knows that it is bitter medicine to be whispered
about and laughed at because he practices, really practices and stands up for his faith.

He knows that it is not easy at work when other men
insist on telling him dirty stories and he shows it is about
as welcome as if they unloaded a garbage truck on his
front lawn or in his living room. He knows that when he
resents it and objects to it he is put down. He only knows
that if he goes to a party where the girls arrive painted
and then get plastered and the whole atmosphere is
pagan and he shows he is uncomfortable, they will want
to know if his halo is on straight or if his wings are not
sticking out. That sort of thing is very easy to ladle out
but very hard to swallow.

And do you know why they ladle it out? Because
deep down under the flamboyant jacket or the shimmering dress they are uneasy about their own conduct and
more than a mite jealous of his. They know it takes
courage to stand alone and be true blue, while anyone
can be yellow and merely follow the crowd. They know
that deep down in their own soul, their conscience is
swinging and ringing like a lighthouse bell, but they do
not want to hear it or heed it, so they try to keep talking
louder and faster and (they hope) funnier. But secretly

they are not heroes to themselves, not by a thousand miles, these loudmouths that scoff at the piety and the purity of others.

Another segment, the self-styled disillusioned young, have shaken the dust of church aisles from loafers and sandals and have sadly turned away because the Church did not turn them on. The Mass was not (pension the poor old adjective!) "relevant." True, in many parishes conciliation was sought via the Folk Mass with humming mini-skirts and strumming guitars, sometimes irreverently referred to as the "Ukulele Eucharist." Trouble is, when they tire of that, what do you do for an encore? How do you trump sanctuary guitars? A trio of sexy saxophones?

The heart of Catholic worship is not the choirloft nor the pulpit but the altar. Not the music (however modern) nor the preaching (however medieval) but the Mass, always interceding for us sinners. The Church, and Catholics of whatever age in the Church, do not worship merely because the ritual is appealing or attractive or "in," but because the majesty of God demands our worship, and the goodness of God deserves it. In the motor-car of religion, worship is not a luxurious and optional accessory. It is the motor itself. It is a necessity. It is an obligation. And the form, basically the Last Supper, is God-given.

Even in the old Tridentine Latin Mass the sacrifice was what mattered. Even for the stolid peasant who merely assisted, it achieved its end, Christ offering Himself for the sins of the world. For those who wanted to understand, there was always the Missal with its crystal meaning. Centuries ago, when the Irish gathered round the Mass Rock, or in our own time when prisoners in a concentration camp huddled in a secret cabin, they knew what they were doing. The last thing they expected of the Mass was entertainment or fascinating interest. They came to give, not to get. At the heart of it was allegiance, expressed in adoration.

As to those who find the homily not to their liking,

because the Church does not face modern issues, but in the old slur "always arrives breathless and too late," it might be well to realize that the Church is not primarily a social institution but a religious one. It aims to remind men to be good, because if men are truly good, the particulars of any community reform will be evident and imperative. Race relations is only a subdivision of love of neighbor. Social justice is the seventh commandment. Situation ethics, on the other hand, is an elastic conscience squirming in a moral bind.

The Church is only divinely established. It is not divinely staffed or administered. It has whole orchards of human faults. It is, however, facing in the right direction. Those who leave it are going the other way. And this applies most of all perhaps to the group that breaks out the flag of righteous anger and maintains they do not go to church *because of all the hypocrites who do.* They will tell you (if you are willing to listen) about Mr. Bourbon who gets stoned every Saturday night but who is still so loyal to the Rock of Peter that he will still go to Mass every Sunday, or these days, every Saturday evening. Or they will tell you about Mr. Ballot, the politician, who has one well-manicured hand in the holy water font and the other in the public till. Or they will tell you about Mrs. Tongue who goes to Mass every single morning but at the same time does a mass-production job in scandal. She gets her gossip wholesale and merchandizes it retail. She has a tongue like an acetylene torch that manages to cut friendships in half with her vicious stories, but the same tongue is tilted toward heaven as she piously says her daily prayers.

This makes the people who have stopped going to church ask triumphantly, "Do you call that, religion?" Of course, those who go to church are supposed to be flabbergasted, humiliated and stopped. Well, the obvious answer is, "No, we do not consider this religion." And what is more important, God does not consider it religion. But do these people really believe that this same God is going to accept the sad fact that hypocrites go to church too, as a valid reason why other people should not go? On judgment day, God is not going to ask us to pass judgment on the deeds or misdeeds of others. When we are in the dock, the spotlight will be entirely upon us. That is why it is good to remember that in the restaurant of this life we pick up the check only for ourselves.

May the good Lord, then, be merciful to those high and mighty ones who in their majesty have decided not to go to church because people whom they consider hypocrites do. Two wrongs do not make a right. Weakness in others gets us no medals as being strong. For any such prodigal son and daughter we pray the gentle Mother of God to open their eyes, and take their hands, and lead them back to a God who is so good that He is willing to forgive even the folly of such as these!

A Pair of Failures

Judas closed the deal on a Wednesday and tradition has dedicated that anniversary to him under the infamous title of "Spy Wednesday." The next night he executed his bargain. That was, of course, Holy Thursday, the evening of the Last Supper, the last supper for Jesus and for Judas. It was also the day of the First Mass, and the supper-table became a communion rail, and the Apostles the first class of First Communicants.

Suddenly Judas slipped away from the rest and plunged out into the darkness that was as black as his plotting heart. A few hours later, while Christ prayed under the whispering leaves of the garden of Gethsemane, the woods about suddenly became alive with the flare of yellow torches and the flash of hostile swords. Out of the ranks Judas stepped forward and identified Christ for the others by pressing on His lips a kiss that must have burned like a branding iron. The betrayal was accomplished.

It is admittedly a pessimistic and a morbid thought, but I never see a class of First Communicants, the softly curved heads of little boys and girls in their childish innocence, but I feel a gripping fear tightening within me. Which one of these will be the Judas? Or which ones? Who among them will betray Christ with a kiss, the kiss of a marriage outside the Church? Who will sell Him for thirty pieces of graft or some dishonest business deal? Who will get up and leave Christ because of coldness and indifference? Who will stay away because the blunt words of another Apostle, a priest, has wounded his pride? Please God, perform a moral miracle. Let not one of these be lost!

Judas never dreamed that our Lord would let Himself be captured and crucified. He had heard Christ prophesy that the Son of Man must go up to Jerusalem and be spat upon and scourged and nailed to a cross, but Judas was sure that Christ would miraculously pass through the midst of His enemies as He had done before. But, when Good Friday dawned, Judas realized the worst was true.

He stumbled back to the temple and flung down his ringing coins and shouted that he had betrayed innocent blood. All he got in reply was a shrug. "Look you to it. It is no concern of ours." They had Jesus; they spurned Judas like the rotten meat that had baited the trap. If Judas had only brought back not his money but his heart; if only he had returned not to the conspirators but to Christ! To Christ even on the cross where the arms were outspread to receive the sinner!

Recently I saw a huge and striking crucifix over the main altar in a new church. The feet alone were spiked to the wood; the arms were off the cross and stretched forward in a circle of love as though to welcome any approaching soul. Palm Sunday ushers in the holiest week of the year. It is the week when the worst of us, we who have betrayed Christ in so many ways, can make our way back to Him. This is the time when the Prodigal Son Express leaves from the mountains of pride or the swamps of sensuality for Calvary, for Christ, for pardon, for peace.

The other great human failure in the crucifixion drama was Pilate. He paced back and forth on his balcony while the wolf pack in the courtyard howled for the blood of the Lamb of God. Jesus stood in the corner, derisively draped in a scarlet cape that did not fall off because the sticky wounds of the scourging held it fast. Suddenly Pilate whirled and silenced the mob with a commanding gesture. They had the privilege, he reminded them, on this outstanding festival to name a prisoner for release. "Whom will you have, Barabbas, (and he named the most unpopular thug in the city) or Jesus Christ?" For a moment there was silence, and then a sullen, rising roar like the pounding of a surf when it has a little ship helpless on the rocks, burst forth, "Crucify Christ! Release Barabbas!"

At that moment Pilate must have hated them to the point of absolute loathing. What must a man do to save the innocent? Few of us realize that Pilate tried five different ploys to rescue Jesus from death. First, he told the Jews he found no true bill in their charge and dismissed the case. Secondly, when they came back he tried for a change of venue and transferred jurisdiction to the Council of the Jews, knowing that under Roman law they had no power to hand down a death-sentence. Thirdly, when the Council craftily refused to hear the case he tried to palm it off on King Herod, feeling that this easy-going playboy monarch would treat the affair lightly. Fourthly, when Herod was miffed that the wonder-worker would perform no miracle for him and sent Christ back, Pilate had Him scourged, hoping thereby to stir the sympathy of the people and make them feel that this was punishment enough. Fifth and finally, Pilate offered to throw to their blood-lust a convicted killer, Barabbas, if they would let Christ go. Again, failure. What more could a man do?

Like most of us, Pilate had one strong weakness. With him it was ambition. He was not afraid of the Jews but he was afraid of Caesar, because Caesar was the man who handed out the patronage. Caesar by a word had made him head of this province; Caesar by another word could drag him back to Rome in perpetual disgrace. Twice before, the Jews had threatened to lodge an official complaint against him with Caesar. Twice he had managed to pacify them. But this was more serious. He could take no chances now. It was a question of his career or Christ, so Christ had to go. Christ and right and honor and justice and truth. Pilate so wanted advancement, prestige, prominence, a permanent place in history. Strangely, too, he got it. Every day millions murmur his name, but it is only like a date on a monument; it only sets the time. "Suffered under Pontius Pilate." His name is written forever in letters of blood in the Apostles' Creed.

Poor Pilate, he could have become the patron saint of justice, and became instead the pattern of the compromising politician who uses situation ethics to control the situation and forget the ethics. But who are we to condemn him so cavalierly? Do we not often try to wash our hands in his silver basin? Pilate could whimper that he did his best before he gave in. When we commit serious sin, do we not often rationalize afterward that the temptation was so strong, or we were so weak, or that we meant no malice, or that somebody led us on? What is all this but Pilate's water that can never wash away responsiblity and guilt?

Only the forgiveness of God can do that, and God forgives only the man who accuses himself, not the man who excuses himself. He forgives not the man who can tick off on his fingers five alibis why he fell, but the man who closes those five fingers into a fist and strikes them against his breast and says from a sorrowing heart, "Through my fault!"

Judas fell through avarice and Pilate through ambition. Any one of us, being human, can fall in any way that any man can. But if we go to Christ on the cross with sincere contrition we shall find that both His hands are raised in absolution.

Shut-In but Not Shut-Out

The other day I picked up an old breviary and out of it fluttered an old holy picture, faded and frayed and with some minute scribbling on the back. It turned out to be the souvenir of a little retreat I had preached many years ago to the nurses of a New England hospital. Written were the names of a few patients, and behind each name a couple of key words so that I would remember the different cases. I find it startling that after all this time the memories come whirring back like the swallows to Capistrano.

Perhaps it is because that hospital was so different. No ambulance ever came whizzing up the drive with siren screaming. There was no tense activity in the emergency room. In fact I doubt if there was an emergency room. Any ambulance that rolled up came with gentle leisurely care. The tip-off to the whole situation was that in the patients' rooms you never saw any of those gay, colorful greeting cards showing toy dogs barking, "Get well soon!"

These people were not going to get well, soon or late, and they knew it. They knew that people went to other hospitals to be cured, but they came here to be made as comfortable as possible before the inevitable end. Once there was carved in grim gray granite over the tall front door, "Hospital for Incurables." Mercifully it has been changed since. The cases are still chronic, and mainly terminal, but the hospital has achieved a reputation as one of the most successful rehabilitation centers in the United States. I was thinking of thirty years ago. Medicine has taken many a giant step in the meantime, but they could never improve the dedication of the hospital personnel or the courage of the patients as I knew them during that brief retreat.

I recall one sweet mother whose white hair puffed out on the pillow behind her like a crown of spun silver. "My trouble," she said softly, "is only a little weakness of the heart. At least that is what they tell me." Then she smiled, and it was like the opening of a gate, and an invitation to come into her confidence. "I know I have cancer. I pretend for the sake of my three sons, and they pretend for my sake. It is all a kind of white lie, but it is done out of love and to spare each other's feelings."

She did have cancer. I checked later. Opposite her in the room across the hall was a rather young woman bent and twisted with arthritis. It was heartbreaking to see the dewy springtime of youth in her face and the rigid and bitter winter in her crippled body. Two nuns, nurses in the white habits, were attending her. One of them had been taking care of such helpless patients in that hospital for almost forty years. The other, who had just been professed, I remembered as a pretty and vivacious nurse who had made a retreat I had preached two years before in a neighboring hospital. Could Communism, I wondered, or paganism (ancient or modern) ever inspire sacrifices like this?

I wandered over to a ward where Tom B. lay on his back with his eyes staring at the ceiling and his body stiff as an ironing-board. His lips were open slightly and it was hard to understand him, yet his eyes twinkled at my little pleasantries and always wore a small smile. It happened to be time for the evening meal, and a nurse began to feed him, ever so gently, pushing a wooden applicator smeared with mush into his vise-like mouth. This had been going on for years and years.

It was not easy to watch, and as I turned away I caught the eye of a fellow at the other end of the ward who was propped up in bed and manfully plying knife and fork over his tray. "Well," I whispered, "they don't have to feed you, do they?" "No, Father. I can't kick." He winked, and waved his fork with a flourish under the tray. "I have no legs." Then he said, "You have to look on the bright side. You see I'm so much better off than the fellow you just left."

The one man I shall never forget, though, was in the next room. He was the brother of a priest, and all but blind, so I had to bend low before he could see me. From his neck down, his body was as immovable as stone. His fingers lay motionless on the sheet like swollen white carrots. What you noticed immediately was the cord draped across his cheek and anchored to one gallant tooth. When he jerked his head (the only thing he could move), it pulled the string that sounded the buzzer at the nurses' station. He was in contact with the world outside his room by a piece of string and a tooth!

These few instances may offer some picture of the affliction and tragedy in that hospital, but they give no idea of the courageous spirit flying over those beds like a banner. We never love God in our vibrant health the way they loved Him in their helpless illness. We never bless God in our sunshine the way they blessed Him in the dark cave of their trial.

There must have been murmurers, rebels, malcontents among them, but I saw none. I had the strange impression that from every pillow there looked up the face of a suffering Christ, and that each bed was a branch office of Calvary. For my money here was the very peak, the Alps of Christlike conduct, because it is so much easier to go around doing good than it is to lie helpless and simply be good. Patient suffering is always harder than active virtue. Harder and more meritorious. It was in that helpless hour when Christ was pinned hand and foot to the cross that He achieved His highest triumph and redeemed the world. In that sense the little string of black beads, wrapped around gnarled and knotted hospital fingers, is a huge cable carrying power that no man can measure and of which the world does not dream.

It was no accident that in this hospital the very central spot is the chapel, with the wings of the building stretching out around it. Stand at the sanctuary and lift your eyes, and the chapel seems to go up and up, and round and round. This is because there are galleries on each floor; this means that the chapel is accessible, without stairs or elevator, by going from any corridor to the corresponding balcony. At the late afternoon Benediction the rolling beds were pushed in, the wheelchairs came creaking along, the crutches came hobbling in and soon the galleries were filled. And as you lifted the golden monstrance in its solemn flashing arc all around that circle of the sick, it was like our blessed Lord in Galilee of old when toward the close of the day they brought to Him sufferers with all manner of diseases. Here, if He did not cure, He certainly consoled. Where else did the sick get their magnificent courage and their serene peace? Shut in they may be, but they certainly are not shut out from the supporting grace of God!

When your little job is done and you leave a hospital like that, you walk lightly down the steps, happy that you can walk. You breathe deep breaths and do not care if it is fumes or dust or smog because it is the outdoors and you are lucky enough to be out there, on your feet and in motion and not shut in. And as you pass down the flower-bordered walk to the gate, two thoughts walk at your side like acolytes. The first is that the people in these hospital beds and wheelchairs who carry their crosses so lightly and nobly, must love God fiercely.

The second thought is this. If ever I am tempted to stand whimpering at the wailing wall of self-pity and feel sorry for myself, let me remember that hospital and those patients, and contrast their endless, bitter sea of suffering with my own trifling eye-dropper of trouble. That should stop the murmuring and turn on a gushing faucet of thanks.

Smorgasbord Christians

There are times when the usually devout Catholic wishes he did not have to turn out for a Sunday Mass, or creep into a humbling confessional, or reach into his wallet to support a parochial school. Being a Catholic seems especially hard at certain random moments, when out of the corner of his eye he observes his non-Catholic neighbor, apparently as upright and as moral as himself, walking in seemingly cushioned comfort along a much more reasonable road to heaven, with none of those steep and stony stretches of obligatory Mass, onerous confession, and the like.

Harder to take, even, is the breezy fellow who acclaims himself a bona-fide Christian but snipes at a Catholic's churchgoing. "Not that I have anything against the Catholic Church, you understand, or for that matter against any church. I just don't see the need of any formal, organized, structured religion. Give me something simple, nothing complicated. Good old Golden Rule, that's my code. 'Do unto others.' Or, I'll settle for 'Love the Lord Thy God, and thy neighbor.' Deeds, not creeds, I always say. Where do you think religion is, anyway, up there on top of the church steeple, or deep down inside a man's heart?"

And so Niagara goes on and on, and since you cannot stop it, all you can do is scoop up a specimen while it roars away. When you analyze the specimen, you find that, like Niagara, this attitude is all wet. Certainly the Golden Rule is a magnificent motto, a superb guide. We cannot stop with the Golden Rule, because Christ did not stop with the Golden Rule. How many of these people who cheerfully insist that the Golden Rule is religion enough, realize that in the very Sermon on the Mount in which Christ proclaimed the Golden Rule He also made five separate references to hell?

Certainly our blessed Lord said, "Thou shalt love the Lord thy God, and thy neighbor as thyself." In doing this He was only capsulizing the commandments for emphasis; He was not cancelling any of them as outdated. If the commandments are ten, no Sinners' Digest can come along and cut them down to one, pigeonholing the other nine. For instance, does not the Third Commandment really say, "Loving God is fine, but don't forget to show that love by keeping holy the Sabbath Day!" So even in the Ten Commandments religion is formal and specific.

Besides, the same God (for Christ is God, the Second Person of the Trinity) has given us in His Scriptures not only the Ten Commandments but also the Seven Sacraments. What about these? Are we to accept the commandments but reject the sacraments? Is the Bible a kind of bulky menu where we can drool over one appetizing item and turn up a wrinkled, disapproving nose at the next? Is Christianity itself a spiritual cafeteria where we push our tray along the gleaming, steaming counter and take what we like and ignore what we don't?

"Heaven? Why, yes, I'll have a heaping helping of that! Everlasting hell? Horrors, no! I couldn't stomach even the thought of it. Baptism? Why, yes. It is quite respectable to be christened, you know. The Mass? Of course not. Confession? Definitely, no. Anointing of the Sick? Not for me!"

Do you really have a choice? Take heaven and hell. There is not one ounce more proof for the existence of

heaven than there is for the existence of hell. We know
about each from only one source, the solemn word of
God. To believe in the one, and not believe in the other,
is thinking with our wishbone and not with our brain,
with our heart rather than with our head.

As to the Mass, what is it but Scripture's Last Supper ("This is My Body. This is My Blood."), repeated
and renewed as Christ commanded ("Do this in memory of Me."). Confession is only remembering that when
He said to the Apostles, "Whose sins you shall forgive,
they are forgiven," He no more meant that this power
was to stop with the Apostles than that the Church was
to stop with the Apostles. It was given to the Apostles
(and their successors) *for* the Church. About Anointing
of the Sick, priest and oils make a vivid picture framed
in that page of Scripture we call the Epistle of St.
James.

These are all sacraments, just as much as Baptism,
and have been accounted sacraments from way back in
the dawn of Christianity when Christian martyrs poured
out rich red blood in their defense. Has a true Christian
a right to by-pass them now? Is Christianity a racing
form where a man checks off his choices? Is it only a gentle, harmless hobby that he pursues according to his own
whims? Is it merely a serene way of spending a Sunday
morning?

By no means. Christianity is religion, and religion is
the debt of worship we owe to God, our Maker, and we
had better pay it. It is the set of rules we get from God,
our Master, and we had better keep them. It is the blueprint from God, the supreme Architect, and if we do not
build according to His plan, we build to our eventual
collapse and our eternal ruin.

Of course any religious rebel can growl, "Simple, interior religion for me. None of this complicated and external show!" But it does not matter what *he* says, if
Christ has said something else. And Christ *has* said, "On
this rock (Peter) I build my Church." And He supple-
mented that by saying of the Church, "He who hears

you, hears me." So it is up to the Church to interpret and develop and carry out the teachings of Christ.

From the beginning the Church was external, from Peter and the Apostles to Paul and the Epistles; from the gatherings of the faithful to the laying on of hands; from the signs of the sacraments, like water, oil, bread, wine, to the Masses said under flickering candles over the tomb-altars of the Catacombs. Religion has to be physical and external because people are physical and external. If we were only souls, then religion too would be invisible, interior, utterly spiritual.

It is easy to sympathize with those who argue that religion has become too complicated. But what organization involving human beings is not complicated? In real estate, searching out a property deed is complicated. In inventions, filing a patient is complicated. In taxes, filling out an income form is complicated. Law, insurance, customs — anything civilized is complicated. A rock is simple because it is only a rock. A wrist watch is complicated because it belongs to a much higher order.

For that matter the United States Army of today is far more complicated than the army of 1776. The picturesque buff-and-blue uniform is now a scientifically tested olive-drab or khaki. The old flintlock musket has become the M-16 or the bazooka or the machine gun. The horse-drawn carts have evolved into jeeps, trucks, tanks. The original quartermaster corps, farmers along the roadside, has become a department that will not recognize a requisition unless it is filled out in triplicate. But, complicated or not, no one will deny that basically this is still the same army, representing the same country, defending the same principles, fighting under the same flag, only with a few more stars.

The Church, too, though more detailed in its legislation and more elaborate in its ceremonial, is still the same Church founded by Jesus Christ, teaching the same doctrines, administering the same sacraments, and governed by the same head, the successor of the original St. Peter. As members of that Church we can no more confine ourselves to the general principle of loving God and our neighbor than a soldier can confine himself to the general principle of serving his country. He soon finds that there are specific orders that regulate the uniform of the day, the way he salutes, the assembling of a weapon, K.P., and those heavenly three-day passes.

We get our regulations from the Church, which gets its authority from Jesus Christ. Sometimes those regulations may seem like a burden strapped to a man's back, awkward, inconvenient, often in the way. But perhaps the fighter-pilot, as he runs toward his plane, feels the same about his parachute. It is a burden too, but it is a precious burden that can save his life. So will our religion save us, and not just the life of the body, but the eternal life of the soul. It came from God and will bring us back to Him.

Through Prison Bars

I had been reading about John the Baptist in the gospels and it was not hard to imagine him with unkempt beard and dark burning eyes, pacing up and down in Herod's dungeon. Then, for no reason at all, some little cell in the mind's computer clicked and switched me to a modern prison I had visited twenty-five years ago. It was during a novena in a Massachusetts town, and out of the sacristy window I could clearly see the great, grim red wall, and on every corner a commanding tower, and in every tower an armed guard. Inside, some nine hundred men, mostly young, were forfeiting some portion of their lives and sacrificing their liberty and a normal pursuit of happiness. A jail is a small-scale model of hell.

Each morning of the novena, the superintendent and his wife came to the early Mass in the town church, and each evening to the novena service. He was a gray-haired, executive type with the erect carriage of a major, as in fact he once had been. One morning after Mass he came into the sacristy and said, "Father, why don't you drop over to see our place? There are a couple of men over there who claim they used to make your novena to Our Lady of Perpetual Help at the Mission Church in Roxbury." I knew we had alumni in many places, but it was a bit disconcerting to think of men who had been making the Nine Wednesdays as now doing nine years.

A day or so later I went over in the afternoon, and was relieved to find that the two men he had spoken of were in uniform and part of the security force. The superintendent asked one of them to take me through the prison. I was glad the prisoners were at work in the shops, because I don't think I would have the heart to walk past human beings in cages. Even empty, the tiers of cells, rising three or four flights, the steel bars, the stone walls and floors, the bareness and the bleakness and the glaring yellow lights, were chilling and depressing. As our footsteps rang out hollowly, I paused before one cell and peered in between the bars. You may not believe it, but there in the dimness I made out a small statue of Our Lady in blue and white. Let me hasten to add that when I looked into the next cell and the next, and next, all I saw was pin-up girls. But what character, grit, courage that one man must have had to enthrone Mary on that dingy shelf as queen of a felon's heart!

And yet, Our Lady seemed at home there. Genuine mother that she is, she would be equally at home in a convent chapel or in a convict's cell. If a good mother has a daughter in the convent, she visits her proudly. If the same mother has a son in prison, she would visit him loyally, even giving him more love, because more was needed. The little statue in the gloom behind the bars seemed to say that if all the world is against you, there is a mother faithful still.

This is especially true of our Mother Mary. It does not matter to her how low a man falls — even if he has dropped so low that his toes touch hell. If he still has faith and sorrow and the will to come back, let him but call up from his dark hole, and Mary will bend down to lift him.

To show such repentance in a jail may take high courage. The chaplain told me that the greatest obstacle in getting the prisoners into the chapel was the shower of ridicule they had to weather for the rest of the day. But is it not the same in what the prisoners call "outside"? Is it not the same in factories or offices or colleges? Try to

be decent in your life, clean in your speech, and hold
high the banner of a practicing Catholic. You will eventually become the target for those who crawl through life
in the mud. But if you are a target for the slurs of the
foul-minded and the filthy-mouthed, take at least this
comfort: the target is not flat in the mud. If it were, it
would never be noticed. No, the target is always high up,
far above the squinting sniper.

Very late that dull and dismal afternoon, I saw the
prisoners returning to their cells. They went stamping
up the stone stairs in rhythmic time, clop-clop, clop-
clop, in deadly unison. The thought whipped through
my mind: if only high school kids could watch this! Not
as a class, for then such youngsters are very brave. They
protest to loathe conformity, but none is quicker to con-
form. If they sauntered through a prison as a group,
there would be the inevitable wisecracks and snickers
and an overall air of "so-what?" Send them through, two
by two, with a hard-nosed guard, then they would come
out thinking some long, long thoughts.

Speaking of high school, the chaplain said that as
far as he knew, not one of the prisoners there had ever
finished a parochial grade school. (Let the nuns of that
generation take a bow!) For that matter, few of them
had ever completed any school. Practically all of them
were the melancholy products of bad or broken homes.
In the game of life, they were called out before they got
to first base. In a grim sense, before they got started,
they were already out *at home.*

It is true they picked pockets, or stole and stripped
cars, or burglarized houses, or held up someone on a
dark street, and were paying their just penalty. But
someone else is guilty too, and someday there will be
another trial before the bar of eternal justice. That day
the sentence of an angry God will fall heavy on a drunk-
en father or a slipshod mother, on a pair of lazy loafers
who kept a dirty home with ragged children whom they
let roam the streets and learn the ways of evil in the very
kindergarten of vice.

I was on the point of thanking the superintendent for his courtesy (though it had been a depressing and heartbreaking visit) when he asked if I wanted to see where he lived. I presumed we would go outside to some house on the grounds, but he surprised me by taking me up one flight and putting his key into what looked like a giant steel wall. A door swung back, and there was a bright, attractive home, with handsome rugs and shining furniture and pleasing pictures. I paused at one small room, close to the metal door, all done in pink and with three large dolls propped against the wall.

"My little girl's" the superintendent said. "She's the youngest, just nine." At that moment, she came bouncing into the room, all smiles and dimples. I could not but marvel that between her childhood innocence and hardened crime there stood only an inch of grey steel wall. But no! Between this little girl and evil stood something stronger than steel: the deep love, the sterling example of dedicated parents. In any family, the best barrier against sin and crime is the devout, decent lives of a good father and mother. Occasionally, a bad child will come from a good home. Occasionally, not usually. By and large good homes produce good people. The strongest impact on the young is not the Church and not the school. It is the home.

We were leaving another room when the superintendent pulled a small key out of his pocket and unlocked the top drawer in a mahogany desk. Carefully he took out what seemed to me to be a sinister handgun, crude and primitive like an old pirate pistol. "It could kill a man," he said. "No question of that. We did some test-firing with it. It was made, secretly of course, in our shops. The trigger works on a spring stolen from a typewriter."

He laid the gun on the table. "One night last year my youngest daughter — you saw her a few minutes ago — came to me and said she wanted to go to Mass the next morning. Our parish Mass here is at seven o'clock. My wife goes almost every morning, but I felt seven is early for the child, so she goes only on Sunday. She pleaded so much this particular night, or maybe the right word is she pestered me so much that I finally gave in, though she could not give me any reason for going that particular day except that she wanted to. According to her, she just had to.

"Next morning when she came back from Mass, she hugged me and kissed me and told me that she had gone to Communion for me and had said a special prayer for me before the Shrine of Our Mother of Perpetual Help at the side altar. Frankly I was puzzled. It wasn't my birthday. Christmas was not near, so she was not trying to butter me up.

"I just shrugged it off and went to work. I wasn't in my office more than an hour when something happened. I was standing at the file cabinet with my back to the door when I felt a gun shoved into my back and a voice snarled, 'Drop your keys on the floor behind you!' If it happened again tomorrow, that is just what I would have done. It's what I should have done. Instead, something made me spring backward, like a back-flip on a diving board. The prisoner went back on his head, the gun — this gun — went sliding along the floor. In an instant, I had whipped out my own revolver and everything was under control.

"But by all the odds I should have been on that floor, dead. A half-hour later, I was still unsteady with shock from the narrow escape and went to lie down for a while. I passed through that room you saw with the dolls. And then I remembered my little girl and how she prayed for me that morning to Our Mother of Perpetual Help. You don't have to preach sermons to convince me of Her power. I know."

Twenty years later, I gave a little mission in that same jail. They told me that just recently Major Dee had died. They don't need a security force in heaven, but they will welcome a man like him.

Teachers Are Great People

When September is a-comin in, and the dusty shades are whirred up from the school windows, and the powdery thud of clapped erasers is heard in the land, it behooves us to think of teachers. To think of them and to thank them. Teachers, to be sure, are not used to being toasted in bubbling champagne. Rather they bend over the water-bubbler and slurp down a few swift gulps, bracing themselves against possible pushers. Incidentally, some classes have fewer cavities because they have fewer teeth.

In our hustling, practical, money-hungry society, teachers have hardly been heroes. Even the youngster senses it. Under the huge billboard that warns: "Drive Carefully! Don't Kill a Child," one of them has scrawled underneath: "Wait for a teacher!" From the cartoonists, too, teachers have had their lumps. The lady teacher is lampooned as a gaunt, angular creature with an aggressive chin like a trowel, steel-rimmed spectacles that could be portholes, a hair-do whose huge ugly knot were better described as a hair-don't, and prim lips pursed as if they were hissing, "Little girls mustn't!"

The male of the sub-species is stroked off as the absent-minded professor, his head lost in the swirling clouds of theory and his feet at the mercy of every mud-puddle in the road or man-hole in the street. What would fiction ever do without the impractical intellectual, tip-toeing through the tulips of his own unrealistic world? Was it Shaw or Kipling who sniped at the dreamy pedagogue: "He who can, does. He who cannot, teaches."

To which success nods an agreeing head and shouts an approving Amen! It must be admitted that if success is measured by the fatness of a wallet, the teacher must bow out abashed. Compared to other professional people, like doctors, lawyers, engineers, architects, the teacher's wallet is not merely flat; it is concave. And I wonder how much it helps, when you are eating hamburger instead of steak, to remember that though teaching is of all professions the poorest paid, it is also the most rewarding? Isn't that the salve generally prescribed for raw teacher-wounds?

When was the last time, or for that matter was there ever a first time, when you said, "Thank you!" to a teacher? The years and the miles separate us, and the gratitude goes unspoken and unwritten. I just hope that this little piece will write off a smidgeon of my debt.

It goes back to the third grade in Our Lady of Perpetual Help School in Brooklyn. Till then my wise mother had decided I was too young to cross the car-tracks along Fifth Avenue. Lest you think my mother with her Leitrim background of cows and sheep was a bit over-awed by modern transportation, let me remind you that the Brooklyn Dodgers were called that, precisely because Brooklynites had to be adept dodgers of that borough's wildly careening trolleys.

Anyway, I was at age eight adjudged to be trusted to look both ways and whip across the rails, and so reach the school. Insecure and somewhat afraid, I was deposited in the classroom of Sister Thomas Mary. She was the first nun I had ever seen at close range, and because she was so pretty and smiling, I fell in love with her on the spot. (Fifty years later, when I happened to give a talk to a regiment of nuns and she introduced herself, I found out that in 1912 she had been twenty.) Her complete kindness made such an impression that I was overwhelmed. If you think I am seeing all this through the glamorous pink clouds of a nostalgia sunset, let me set down that I also remember it was a nice neighbor, Mrs. Scott, who brought me to be enrolled, and that on the way home she bought her son, Walter, and me a walnut ice cream cone. Walnut! I remember it well!

Why is it that I remember those nuns of so long ago, I who cannot remember the names of people I met yesterday? Let the good, dedicated teachers hug this to their hearts: they do make a deep impression. I can still see Sister Constantia, the principal, standing on the stoop of the schoolyard, like an admiral on the quarterdeck, and swinging her authoritative bronze bell. At its first clashing bong we froze, scarcely daring to set down a leg the bell had caught in mid-air. And there was Sister Eduardo, who schoolyard scuttlebut never doubted was a full-blooded Indian, though I later found out her swarthy profile harked back to the Spanish Irish, a living footnote to the Armada. When she strode down our seventh grade aisle, a rustling, clicking tower of black and white, and glared at you from under her bonnet like a dark, hooded eagle, and abruptly stopped, and tapped her menacing toe on the wooden floor and slowly bit out, "Master Manton!" every syllable sounded like the blow of a judge's gavel sentencing you to Siberia.

Later on, when I looked back and remembered how she used to have us come to school an hour before the regular day, that is at eight instead of nine, to prepare us for the fearsome New York State exams called the Regents, I realized how her whole life was centered around her pupils. When I surprised her and got a hundred, she shook my hand. That was in June. In September she had to begin all over again with another group. This must be the hardest thing about being a teacher. You never climb to the top of a mountain. You just keep going up and down a flight of stairs.

How easily the strange names come back, after
more than a half-century! Sister La Salette. We always
figured she was a distant relative of the French explorer,
La Salle, whom we studied in her geography class. She
never denied it. Sister Cor Joseph. It means heart of
Joseph. We always thought it was Cord Joseph, and had
something to do with the black cord the Sisters of St.
Joseph wore to support their long tinkling rosary. And
Sister Marita. She was short and slim, like a six iron,
and showed some of her eighth graders the fastest left
jab in Brooklyn, with the possible exception of Benny
Leonard. She made high school easier by giving us
classes in elementary Latin and algebra.

Of lay teachers we had only two, but they ran the
same taut ship, and commanded the same respect, either because of their own dominating personalities, or
because the all-pervading awe of the nuns washed over
the whole school. Certainly Miss Furey needed neither
veil nor wimple to establish discipline. One day when we
massacred an unexpected arithmetic test, she folded the
big foolscap papers into little hats, wrote our names on
each in huge red crayon, and marched us slowly up and
down the aisles of two classrooms of snickering girls. I
can still feel the fire in my face.

There were sterner pupil standards perhaps in those
days, but the mark of the good teacher never changes.
Call it dedication, or interest, or involvement, it is a
complete giving over of oneself to the job at hand. As in
any other profession, a good teacher is one who lives his
life and loves it, eats and breathes his subject, and almost hates the clock. Who was it said that the ideal university was two men on a log, one eager to teach and one
willing to learn? In the days when the old gray mare clip-
clopped down Main Street, the old saying was that you
could lead a horse to water but you could not make him
drink. George Ade parodied it with, "You can lead a
man to college but you can't make him think." The real
teacher can, or at least he can make the student want to.

Communication is the key. Communication and in-

spiration. After all, most of the facts are in the textbook.
The teacher is not supposed to be just a kind of human
crane loading a child's mind with decimals and dates
and the capitals of the Carolinas and the exports of
Ecuador, the way a ship is loaded at a dock. At least not
in the higher grades. Here is where the enthusiasm
comes in, leading the young mind down the corridor of
learning into vast and glittering rooms he would eventually explore.

It would be pedagogical heresy, to be sure, to say
that knowledge is the least part of a teacher's equip-
ment. Still, what sets the great teacher apart and lets
him light up a classroom the way a great actor lights up
a stage, is not information but communication. In fact
some cynic has remarked, "The ideal teacher is part
actor, part preacher, and if added to this he has scholastic qualities, he is a rare bird indeed."

They cannot be too rare, though, because whenever
a little knot of us get to discussing great teachers we
have had, everybody seems to recall three or four favorites. This is true whether the group is busy drowning
olives at a cocktail party or stabilizing standards at a
priest's retreat. I think of Father Martin Gounley who
first introduced us to philosophy and made us feel like
one of Balboa's *conquistadores,* standing on a lofty peak
and gazing out for the first time at the glimmering ex-
panse of the Pacific. How thrilling this newly discovered
world of thought! "My mind to me a kingdom is!"

At Catholic University it was Dr. Arthur Deering
who looked like something Central Casting would send
out in response to a call for a Supreme Court justice. The
silver mane, the carved bronze profile, the bell-like
booming voice — he was made up for life to stand under
a spotlight. He used to come into the classroom as
though he had just swung off a horse, and toss his hat
toward some indefinite chair, blissfully careless of
whether it hit the mark or not. Then he would spread out
before him the broad pages of his folio-like volume of
some Shakespearean play, and from that moment he,

and we, were in the Elizabethan world. He had all the footnotes filed in his brain, but they never smothered the fire in his heart. With him at the desk we saw Shakespeare at it rang from the stage of the original Globe, not as it was embalmed in some dreary glossary.

The flag of my homage dips lowest in tribute to the obscure, unappreciated, taken-for-granted primary teachers whose thankless task it is to coax young people through the drudgery of getting the fundamentals! The freckle-faced lad tugging impishly at the pigtails that hang over his desk, the ink-stained note surreptitiously passed across the aisle, the classroom panorama wriggling like a can of restless worms and sometimes about as fragrant, and over all this the necessary repetition, like the boring scales of piano exercises — the lady who stands in front of this day after day is the lady who holds a lamp as high and bright as any Statue of Liberty.

Let her (or his) consolation be this. Part of you flies with every pilot, builds with every architect, diagnoses with every doctor. Because you have not lived remote and aloof on the top rung of a library ladder, but have made your way into the mind and heart of the little ones, you are part of them. And if "of such is the kingdom of Heaven," will you be a stranger there?

Heroes and Heroines of the Humdrum

The other day I opened an old seminary notebook and a small time-yellowed clipping floated to the floor. I had scribbled across it, "Brooklyn Tablet, 1928." That was the year before I was ordained. The whole story consisted of but one single sentence that read: "Rev. John Riesacher, S.J., former Novice Master of St. Andrews on the Hudson, has sailed for the Philippines where he will work among the lepers."

I feel certain that up to the moment when I had scissored that item I had never heard of Father Riesacher. I am sure that I have never heard of him since. Why, I wonder, did I snip that one-sentence space-filler and mean to keep it? I think I remember. For one thing the simplicity of the "Bon Voyage" no doubt impressed me. There was no photograph, no farewell party, no fanfare at all. But even beyond that I believe I sensed a kind of general injustice.

Mention "priest among the lepers" to the ordinary Catholic and what picture fills the TV screen of his mind? Father Damien. Nobody but Father Damien. Here was a hero, I grant you, an apostle of the hopeless, and eventually even a martyr to his own obscure crusade. Thanks to Robert Louis Stevenson he did not remain obscure long. Now, when a Catholic hears of a leper colony his mental computer briskly whisks out the card, Damien of Molokai. To people in general, there is one Niagara, one Sahara, one Alps, one Grand Canyon, one Shakespeare, one Michelangelo — and the second row never quite gets into the picture. There the camera of recognition goes fuzzy and begins to blur. Headlines for the heroes, but for the also-rans only oblivion.

Say leper colony and who would ever think of Father Riesacher? Only some lepers, and God. In the intervening years, I have come to know a saintly Irish Redemptorist who is also giving his life to the lepers in the Philippines. I know him but you can be sure that history will never know him. The trumpets of fame will never blow taps over his out-of-the-way grave. Does it matter? God knows. God rewards. The rest is gift-wrapping. Sometimes the realization of this may help you, if you have been, for example, a faithful member of a large city parish for many years and have contributed generously to its support, and have responded to its every appeal, and yet have never been recognized or spoken to by one priest. Welcome to apostolics anonymous!

In a way it reminds me of those two French priests, the Curé d'Ars and the Abbé Bailey. It would be almost impossible to write a dull biography of the Curé d'Ars. The supernatural and the preternatural peer unexpectedly and eerily through the window on so many rustling pages. Most fascinating of all (at least to this reader) is the remote and shadowy figure in the background without whom the Curé d'Ars could never even have become a priest. The biographers almost ignore him. In the life of a great wonder-working canonized saint, who cares about plain Father Bailey?

It is often forgotten that only after the Curé d'Ars was ordained did he manifest that deep wisdom by which he could write out precisely the right prescription for every spiritual problem. Only then did he reveal the discerning insight that could cut like a scalpel into the heart of the matter. But, as in the creation of the world, so it was with the Curé. In the beginning there was only

chaos and darkness. When young John Baptist Vianney
(that was his family name) shuffled off the farm in his
boxcar shoes and into the village school, he led the other
lads in age but in learning trailed them like a caboose. In
secondary school he still inched along like a student
snail with each new lesson looming up like an impassible
and impossible alp. In the preparatory seminary he at
least showed consistency, ranking last among two
hundred. He was admitted to the major seminary only
because of the dean of admissions (who saw the youth's
unusual piety and somehow surmised his great common
sense) looked the other way. He was dismissed from the
seminary eventually when the matter-of-fact rector
caught up with the young man's weird grades, looked
him in the eye and said: "My dear boy, wherever your
place is, it is not here!"

So the slow youth glumly betook himself away from
the seminary building but not from the seminary books.
Now he studied in a rectory. Studied, studied, studied.
Finally he took exams for another diocese, and by what
some might consider a minor miracle (by sheer accident
he was interrogated on the only points he knew), God
blurred the eyes and melted the heart of the presiding
bishop, and the plodding student was at last admitted to
ordination.

Once through that golden door, he was soon ap-
pointed pastor of the village of Ars and was eventually
canonized as St. John Vianney, whose feastday is August 4th, whose statue or picture adorns so many rec-
tories and whose priestly life was so perfect and whose
pastoral life was so fruitful that he has been officially
designated as the patron of all secular clergy. Nobody
has ever designated Father Bailey as anything. He too
was an extraordinarily holy man even to the secret wearing of a hairshirt. That was a minor penance. This was
the man who endured more than five years of torture as
St. John Vianney's voluntary tutor, the man who took
into his own home the awkward, groping, stupid youth
that nobody wanted, and who spent thousands of hours

in the dry martyrdom of feeding him knowledge one grain at a time. Even when the future saint himself wanted to quit and go back to the farm, Father Bailey pleaded with him and prevailed on him to grip the book harder and forget the plow-handles. There never would have been a famous Curé d'Ars if there had not been an obscure Father Bailey. But does he ever get any credit?

So often it is that way in life. Wherever you have a "big wheel" whirling in its prominent arc, there is often an unrecognized little wheel turning even faster to keep the big one in motion. Our consolation is that God sees all the little wheels. God's glance moves swiftly from the beribboned commander with his rows of tinkling medals to the weary foot-soldier slogging along with no badge but blood and mud. God's eye goes from the smart trim pilot of the great silver plane to the grease-monkey in his smeared and spattered over-alls who keeps it flying. God's gaze travels from the professional man with his gilt-edge success to the sister or brother in the family whose sacrifices opened the path to his career. And how often God's eye leaves the preacher in the pulpit with his enameled phrases to rest lovingly on the humble lay brother in the sacristy quietly saying his beads for the success of the sermon. It is those beads that persistently beat on the sinner's heart like raindrops drumming on a roof. It is not the thunder of the preaching but the lightning of grace that strikes the listener's soul. Like a good shopper, the Lord knows values.

It is inevitable that in life a great many people have to play what the world calls second-fiddle. Take out the second-fiddles and where is your orchestra? It is enough if each of us realizes that his duty is to play *his* instrument, follow his own score and never lose sight of the conductor, God. Let the soloists have their solos. Even in our Lord's day it was the Apostles who led the parade and got the salute of palm branches. The poor disciples, undistinguished and unacclaimed, marched over the backroads of history into oblivion, but, let us also hope, into heaven, which is really all that matters.

In our time, too, the majority must always be people who never know reporters and write-ups, never encounter photographers and flash-bulbs. They are the little people, the small beads on God's rosary of friends. Dear to the heart of God must be, for example, the heroic wife who keeps together a little family despite a husband who is a sodden and useless and helpless as a cork fallen into a bottle of whiskey. Dear to God must be the brave young girl who cheerfully closes the blinds on bright romance in order to take care of an aged parent or perhaps younger brothers and sisters. Dear to God in a special way the parents who have done their level best to bring up their children in a Christian manner, only to find that one of them, after all their care and devotion, like a gun that backfires, suddenly explodes in their faces, and they find themselves wounded and scarred by the misdeeds of their very own. Dear to God must be all the quiet heroes and heroines of a humdrum life who go on loving God and helping their neighbor while all the time they go on carrying the heavy load of a broken heart!

The ordinary garden-variety of Christian who may not have a pretentious house but who is the head of a little, happy God-fearing home; the man who may not have on his wall a college diploma attesting how much he knows but who does have in his soul a humility acknowledging how much he needs God; the sinner who after a fall does not shrug his shoulders and blame his glands or heredity or environment, but strikes his breast and murmurs: "Through my fault!"; the churchgoer who looks up to the Lord for the strength to be good but also looks around at his neighbors for chances to do good — such a one, though he be completely unknown beyond the tiny island of his own family and friends, though he live as quietly as a fruit-bearing tree and go to his grave as simply as the planting of a seed, surely must have waiting for him a high place in heaven and at mention of him name angels must smile.

Some day Our Lady herself, who all her life stood in

the background, behind the highly-publicized Herods and high priests and Pilates and Pharisees, will escort him to his proper place in the front rank of God's favorites, the little people that the calculating world dismissed as insignificant but that He loved best of all!

First You Have to Forget

Periodically someone announces that the two most beautifully sounding words in the English language are "cellar door." I do not know the other entries in this verbal derby but I shyly suggest that the three hardest English words to pronounce may well be, "I forgive you." Not even St. Blaise and the blessing of the throats can wrench these out of some people.

Curiously this reluctance to forgive is not too rare among otherwise pious persons. It is something you might never suspect, like the attraction that diamonds have for grease. In a diamond mine excavated earth is sent sliding down a chute to a kind of separator-table. The surface of this table is thickly coated with grease. Clay and pebbles go gayly skidding across the scum, but a diamond will stick to it.

So you have men and women who in their moral lives are pure as diamonds but who get strangely entrapped in the slime of hate. Somewhere along the line of life they have been wronged, and mentally they cannot get past that spot. They have been hurt and they will not forgive. They will not forgive because they cannot forget. They go on munching the grudge as if it were fudge. They will not swallow their grievance like most normal people. They keep chewing it like a cow with a cud.

Events of long ago, but only memories now, are like sunshine: they can warm or they can blister. They can drag down or lift up. There is a certain religious order of men that has in its novitiate a so-called relic room. Each day the novices passing through can see mounted on the wall the savage sword that was plunged into one of their priests in a South American village. Next to it hangs the blunted Mongolian club that splattered another missionary's brains over a China road. Next to that a glasscase frames the bloodstained shirt of a third martyr, not the less touching because time has darkened the scarlet spots to a rusty brown.

When the cassocked young men file through that room and glimpse these grim trophies on the wall they are not incited to hatred or let down to discouragement. On the contrary, off that sacred wall blows a mysterious breeze that stirs the flame of their courage and keeps it alive. They feel that they too must do great things for God, or if necessary even suffer great things for Him, like these holy heroes who have so gallantly pioneered before them.

Contrast this with a man whose heart is a museum of black and bitter memories, who lives surrounded by framed reminders of the wrongs he has suffered, the insults he has endured, the advantages taken of him. Here the smell of self is all over the place. Here he broods among memories that do not inspire but incite, memories that do not glow but that scorch and char. They turn inward like a suicide's dagger.

In greater or lesser scale we all can find ourselves in this surly, growling lair. We recall something that happened to us and a black thundercloud drops down over our heart. Our soul scowls and our temper hates. What was the last crisis that had your heart grinding its teeth? Was it that promotion at the office that you honestly deserved but from which you were trickily swerved? Or was it a loud snub at a quiet party? Was it a favor you humbly asked but were coldly refused? Was it the shabby deal you got in Aunt Farina's will? Was it — or is it — the present thankless attitude of a son or daughter, a cruel ingratitude that Shakespeare compares to a vulture chained in the heart and pecking away day and night?

Whatever it is or was, nobody is trying to minimize the wrong. I am only trying to emphasize that we are guilty of a second wrong if we do not forgive. Surely in God's eyes we were not to blame if we were the ones insulted or mistreated, but equally surely on God's lips is the injunction that we must grant forgiveness to others if we expect forgiveness ourselves.

How can we forgive if we plant ourselves so often before the TV set of memory and darkly watch re-runs of the old grievances? How can that fire of resentment die down if we keep tossing on fresh logs? There is even the danger that our attitude toward any particular gripe will turn irrational, possibly psychotic. I remember reading one time about a woman who dwelt a couple of thousand miles from New York's Metropolitan Opera House but who lived for the radio broadcasts of the opera on Saturday afternoons. A patron has to have a well-upholstered wallet to buy a ticket for an orchestra seat at the Met, but this lady did not just buy the ticket, she actually bought the seat. When the opera house was being refurbished she had one of those old seats shipped out to her. On Saturday afternoons she would don her black velvet gown and the strands of pearls and sink into the faded red plush and peeled gilt of her orchestra seat and listen to the radio as if it were all happening right in front of her.

And that is exactly what some of us do with our old grievances. We are continually running up the curtain again and restaging them as if it were going on now, and out there in the dark we glare and smolder and fume and mentally curse and yearn to bite off a sweet chunk of revenge. Obviously this is the last way to persuade ourselves to forgive. In this respect the fifth commandment is precisely like the sixth commandment. One commandment may forbid hate and the other impurity, but the best way to fight either is to leave the battleground. One arouses fury and the other lust, but the tactics against both are the same: you rip down from the wall of your imagination or your memory the picture that stirs the passion.

Incidentally nobody is claiming that it is an easy thing to wave out of your mind a genuine injustice, a heart-scalding insult, a calculated and malicious wrong. It would be dandy if we could simply open the top-floor window of our memory and drop the incident. But maybe it has been a boarder there — and a brooder too — all these months or even years, and emphatically does not want to leave. As unlikely a moralist as Mark Twain observed that there are some habits that we have to lead downstairs step by step, and even then they occasionally break away and dart up the stairs again.

In other words with the best of resolutions the best of us can fail. So we strike our breast, roll up our sleeves and begin again. Right beneath the rectory window where these lines are being written hangs a bronze plaque testifying that on this site the old Brindsley Mansion stood, and testifying that while George Washington may not have slept here he at least held conferences here. Just at that time, right after the Battle of Bunker Hill, he had drummed out of the Revolutionary Army a Captain John Callendar of the Massachusetts Militia. The charge was arrant cowardice. Callendar marched out of that court-martial with his dishonorable discharge to the camp of another regiment and enlisted as a private. One year later, at the Battle of Long Island, he fought with such spectacular and resourceful bravery that Washington cancelled the old conviction and on the spot restored him to his former rank.

The moral is that anyone can falter and fall, but nobody need stay down. We may lose a battle, but we never make a truce. We go back to the fight! So when we find ourselves brooding over the wrongs done us in the past, leafing through the faded pictures in that album of bitter memories, running our finger over the scars of ancient grievances, the only thing to do is to force ourselves to think of something else, to swing the telescope of our mind on an opposite quarter of the sky. Even if we start thinking about the sales tax, or the income tax, or the excise tax, and the gauge of our temper begins to rise, at least it is impersonal. One thing is sure. In any incident involving our neighbor (or what is often worse, a relative) we must resolutely close our memory like a closet and forget, before we can hope to open our heart and forgive.

On the scales of God, almsgiving is good, but forgiving is better. In fact we have no choice. Not everybody can give alms, but everybody has to forgive. Peter's Pence here becomes millions. Poor Peter's jaw must have dropped when he found out there was no limit in this matter of forgiveness. "How often must I forgive? Seven times?" And the Lord looked him in the eye and said, "Seventy times seven times!" But then what would you expect of the gentle and generous Christ who died with both bloody hands raised in absolution and with parched lips murmuring over a whole world: "Father, forgive them, for they know not what they do."

Battles without Banners

In the colorful mural of American history one of the most exciting panels is the settling of the western section of Oklahoma. It was a bargain-counter rush, and the bargain was land, the land that had not been assigned to the Indians. That April day in 1889 thousands upon thousands of new settlers lined up along the Kansas border like a long curling wave posed for the crashing break and the swirling overflow.

They were a rough and tough crowd, pioneers and adventurers, fighting to be in front and so get the best parcel of land. Dogs barked, men shouted, horses reared, wagons strained at the ready, eager to lurch off. They had to stand back of a certain line, and to insure this the United States Cavalry was strung out in front, riding grim patrol. Then, at high noon, the army bugles blasted out all along the seething strip, and with a great roar the rush was on! Ride like the wind, choose your land, pound down your stakes, guard your claim with your gun! So in part Oklahoma started out like a wild stampede and grew to a glorious state.

This unique incident in American history is in its way the picture of each man's conscience, except that we must never let the rush get started. Along the borders of every human soul, animal passions are forever lined up, a restless, wild, crowding mob, eager to take over. Green-eyed envy is there, and anger red with rage; dishonesty with its long, clutching fingers; hatred with its hard, haughty face that refuses to forgive; impurity whose eyes are mud-puddles and whose hands are slimy claws; hypocrisy, always ready to pull down the mask and live a lie; yawning sloth that puts morning prayers or even Sunday Mass last on the list of priorities; all these and so many other evil tendencies and passions push and strain on the edge of every soul. But they cannot cross the line, they cannot take over one foot of domain unless our own free will, our own deliberate choice, first sound the bugle of consent.

Therein lies the majesty of being a man, the glory of being a human being! Our passions are subject to our will-power. All civilization is built on that solid foundation, that every man has free will and self-control — if he wants to use them. Those who cannot or will not, we put in mental hospitals or in jails. After all, this is the deep and broad chasm that lies between a man and an animal. On the one side stands the animal with his raw, savage impulses, like an unbroken stallion. On the other stands man with his admitted passions, but he is like a spirited horse governed by a rider with reins and bit to maintain control.

We hear of all kinds of control. We hear of price control, flood control, rent control, birth control, but the brightest campaign ribbon on humanity's uniform, as it has fought its way upward, is self-control. Show me the man who is not blown about by any wind of temptation, like a leaf in a gale, but who has complete control over his passions like a plane pilot at his instrument panel, and I'll show you a great man. It is true that the world claps its hands along the routes of presidents and kings; it showers blizzards of ticker-tape on returning heroes; it goes after the autographs of famous actors and actresses; it sits patiently in the outer offices of gilt-edged financiers. In a word it salutes wealth and fame and beauty and power.

But, as God views things from the balcony of heaven, all these earthly successes may very well be like toys scattered on a nursery floor. In the scales of God the only real greatness is goodness. History calls one man Alexander the Great. Alexander may have carved out kingdoms with a sword as a man might cut a wedding cake, but this is the same Alexander who in a drunken rage went completely berserk and ran that sword through his best friend. With that bleeding corpse at his feet do you think he was truly Alexander the Great? In the books of God he may well have gone down as Alexander the little, the weak, the nothing.

Greater far in the eyes of God is the man or woman who fights and wins the wars of temptation on the battlefield of the soul, those secret, lonely wars that nobody knows about. Will it not be strange if judgment day reveals how many a pure, quiet slip of a girl, frail as a flower, had self-control like a taut wire, and character firm as bronze, while some of the headline names of history in their own moral struggles had no more strength of will than a shaky blob of yellow gelatin? Such a man, to steal a comparison from Shakespeare, is like a flute that the devil can pick up whenever he wishes and play whatever tune he wills.

Why should we make an effort to control our passions? Why not let yourself go? That is what the world whispers and the weakling is too eager to agree: "It's in me. I can't help it." The heavy drinker says *he* can't help it. The light lover says *he* can't help it. The man with the volcanic temper says *he* can't help it. But suppose a man gets an urge to throw bricks through store windows and tells the judge, "I can't help it," how far will he get? By the same token, if we have the urge to start throwing bricks through the commandments, and try to tell the Judge of judges, the Judge from whom there is no appeal, that we can't help it either, will not the straight answer be that with the grace of God and our own determination we *can* help it? When a trolley goes careening down a steep grade and crashes off the track, the motor-

man may be able to say with honest truth, "My brakes
did not work." But the brakes of the human will always
work, if we bear down on them hard enough.

Most of us are weak in one or the other department
— what the theologians call our predominant passion. Otherwise we think we have remarkable self-control. But is not
this like saying that we are proud of being strong where it
does not take any particular strength to be strong? Or why
boast of a fine set of teeth if one of them is abscessed? Isn't
it better to take care of the bad one?

The devil knows our particular weakness and he is
going to play our weakness like a fisherman plays a fish.
I remember once while giving a novena in northern Ver-
mont, seeing a fisherman who was the complete angler.
He stood in the stream with hip-boots, between a series
of foaming white falls and some dark quiet pools. Stuck
around his hat-band he had a whole parade of feathered
flies, and hidden inside each feather was a murderous
little hook.

The trick, it seems, is to know which particular in-
sect is hatching in that particular stream and at that
particular time (the best way is to cut open a fish and
find out what has been on his bill of fare) and then to
choose an artificial fly that will make the trout think it is
one of those insects. So the fisherman may select something vivid like a Royal Coachman or something dull
like a Gray Ghost. Anything to fool the fish.

Do you think the devil is less clever in drifting a
special bait toward the sinner? I am not sure that he has
fancy items like Royal Coachmen or Gray Ghost but he
certainly does have lures like Alcohol Glow, Easy
Money, Willowy Blond, Sweet Revenge, Black Spite,
and a dozen others. And you can be sure that he will
always dangle the right bait before the right person,
playing his or her weakness. The trouble is that we think
we can nibble at the edges of temptation and somehow
keep away from the hook, the sin. In nine cases out of
ten, self-control does not mean staying there and fighting the temptation (that would be like a fish trying to

bite the hook in half) but self-control really dictates getting out of range completely and at once.

This naturally takes spiritual energy. It means struggle. And, that, alas, is the story of this world as a place of trial. Eternal rest and perpetual light come later. We shall enjoy the eternal rest, and the perpetual light will shine upon us, if we ask Our Lady's help. Through that help, which is the grace of God given us through Mary's gentle hands, we shall have strong self-control over our passions, and God's flag will fly victorious over the lonely battlefield of our soul.

Lift Up Your Hearts!

The older we grow the more we realize that as human beings we are different only in minor details; in major matters we are very much alike. Each one of us is only a different wave in the same ocean. One wave may be a gentle ripple, and another a foaming billow, but the water in each is identical. And, if there is one trait that is as common to us all as salt is to the sea, it is a tendency to grow discouraged, to lose heart, to plod the shadowy trail of glum depression.

"I am alone and afraid . . . in a world I never made." Who has not thought that? Like children we are all afraid of the dark, only it is the dark memories of past sins or the dark mystery of the impenetrable hereafter. We find no joy in prayer; we try, but our mouth is filled with dust and ashes. We strain to believe, but faith becomes a dim tunnel that stretches on with no lights ahead. We feel drawn toward the glitter of temptation, and we know that only a thread holds us back.

All of which proves that we are not angels nor card-carrying members of the communion of saints, but struggling human beings whose hearts so often sink into our boots. Perhaps this is precisely why the wise old Church says or sings in every Mass of the year, "Lift up your hearts!"

Why lift up our hearts? Because God loves us despite everything. Many years ago an enterprising photographer set this sign in his window: Your Photo at Your Own Price — As you look to me: $5; As you think you look: $10; As you would like to look: $15.

God sees us as we are, and He still loves us. Not our sins, but us, even our poor human nature that falls and that looks up from the dirt pleading to be set on its feet again for another try. No matter what mud is smeared across our soul's white baptismal robe, no matter how long we have lived as guests in the devil's villa of sin, as long as we are still alive with breath in our lungs and resolve in our hearts, we are souls to be saved, candidates for heaven, and important and precious to God.

We ought to know this, but we forget. How is it that we can forget? If ever we were shut up in a communist prison and lingered and languished there, and one day were suddenly set free, we would never forget the rattle of the jailer's key as it opened our cell. If ever we had been entombed in a mine after a cave-in, and been miraculously rescued, we would never forget the thud of the pick and the scrape of the shovel that broke through to reach us. A rescue like this did happen to us once, and the sound we should never forget is a hammer clanging down on iron spikes. The executioner did not know it, but he was tapping out in the code of the cross, "See, He dies to set you free!" That is how much the Lord loves us. Sometime quietly lay your hand against a post or a tree and think of a spike crashing through it, and you hanging by those hands, bleeding and fighting for breath (the end of crucifixion is choking to death) and you will realize how much He loved you.

The part to remember is that our blessed Lord died not for your good qualities, not for your beauty or your brains or your sunny disposition or your virtues, but for your sins, your faults. So, what honor do you pay Him if you trust His mercy only when you feel innocent and sure and unstained? A hospital is for the sick, and the sicker a man is, the more right he has to be in the hospital. God's mercy is the hospital for sin. So, don't say to Him with your lips, "Lord, be merciful to me a sinner," and then by the distrust in your heart bring up a thimble or an eye-dropper for your forgiveness. His generosity is measured by our trust.

And do not think that this is all well and good for the saints. They can talk about the boundless mercy of God, because they really don't need it. They look at their tiny faults through magnifying glasses and convince themselves they have an attic full of broken commandments. Their ideals are so high that when they look down at their life they think they have a soul like a city dump. Instead, consider someone who really was a sinner. Would you settle for Mary Magdalen? She was scorned by the Pharisees. She was branded as a public sinner. Her soul was a blotch of moral scabs and blistered sores. Her past could be wrung out like dirty water from a grimy and greasy mop. Yet on Easter morning when He left the tomb the Savior sought her out first. Could there be a greater guarantee of forgiveness? Was not this the very Christ who had said, "Let not your heart be troubled nor let it be afraid!"

That same Christ waits for us, not at the tomb, but in the confessional. For what is the Church, what are the sacraments but the extension of Christ into our day, the contemporary Christ among us now? In the confessional there shines His bright forgiveness so that in a few moments all the black slush of sin goes gurgling down the gutters of conscience, leaving the soul radiantly white.

And if God forgives us, should we not also forgive ourselves? Otherwise are we not setting ourselves up a higher court than that of heaven? This is not virtue. This is insolent and arrogant pride.

Sin is not the only dark pine that throws its sinister shadow across our heart. As human beings, suffering is the badge of all our tribe, and everything from business reverses to poor health to unrequited love can send the bitter waters of sadness rolling through our soul. Some people are natural optimists and can meet such setbacks by telling themselves that the darkest hour is just before the dawn, that the tide of trouble reaches its high point and then has to turn, that life is a see-saw, and when it hits bottom, it immediately starts pushing toward the top. There may be some truth in this cheerful stance and there certainly is helpful encouragement. We need not only natural but supernatural aid. It is surely true that God fits the burden to the back. Our job is to muster the courage to face the burden. This we can get if we ask it earnestly of God.

How many have found that out by a daily visit to a church! Years ago a storekeeper opposite a downtown church asked me, "Why do people drift in there all day long, even when there is nothing special going on?" I felt like answering him in the words of the Apostle about Christ. "Come and see!" The fact of the matter is that in the quiet of a church many of us do feel a nearness to God, and we leave with the courage to go back to the fight!

So, if ever the panic bell rings furiously through your soul, and you feel like moaning that all is lost, remember it never can be so bad as that, as long as you can turn to God. Some years back, a certain nun (call her Sister Gorgonzola) was transferred from a popular academy. At once the other sisters were in high dismay. "Why Sister Gorgonzola is our best teacher, our finest organizer, our greatest all-around talent!" That night pious bonnets shook in consternation, and starched wimples were wet with tears. But mother superior, who was not only a rock of common sense but a very quarry of it, pointed out gently, "It is true, Sisters, that Sister Gorgonzola is leaving us. But please remember, she is not taking with her the key to the tabernacle."

No tragedy is ever the end of the world, though something like the loss of a dear one or the breaking of an engagement can send a person reeling. No setback is so drastic that it takes away our blessed Lord and His helping grace. Against His Sacred Heart we can rest our grieving heart. From His loving kindness our weakness can always draw strength.

Sane View of Sex

Although there are canonized married saints like St. Monica and St. Elizabeth of Hungary and St. Thomas More (who was married twice), some people seem to believe that the Church is secretly lobbying to repeal sex. Why? For almost a score of centuries the Church has had a box seat, front and center, for watching the parade of life pass by. During that long span she has witnessed all sorts of changes. She has seen spears become guided missiles, togas become topcoats, chariots become dragsters, and the hooded monk huddling over his copying desk evolve into a swishing duplicating machine. While all along the line things have changed, people have not. Men and women are still men and women. So why should the Church ever deny the necessity of sex, the popularity of sex, the universality of sex? How could she pretend to ignore it or sighingly wish it would go away?

For where did sex come from? From the Creator, God. True, there always have been, perhaps, some prudish people (in and out of the Church) who shake their heads and wonder how the Deity ever brought Himself to start this intimate process of procreation. It almost seems as if the Lord got involved in something indecent in sponsoring so awkward an arrangement. Perhaps it would be better to look vaguely across the street, hum a tune, and think of something else. It is all so indelicate.

The Catholic Church has never preached that God turned away with an embarrassed blush from the marriage bed. On the contrary, she has always insisted that physical pleasure is not of its nature shady, shocking, nor shameful, but rather wholesome, noble, and meritorious, provided it represents not simply a union of bodies like the mindless matings of beasts, but a union of hearts and minds and personalities. She also insists, that to protect children and the rights of others, sex must be restricted to a union under the sacred canopy of marriage.

There are three things to emphasize in discussing sex, and the first is that sex tends to be overemphasized. Those who beat the drum for absolute sexual freedom, open-season promiscuity, lust on the loose, are just as misguided, at their end of the spectrum, as the mythical Victorian who would like to believe that sex did not exist. The truth is in between. Sex is a department of life, but it is not the whole of life. It is an important stone in the mosaic of living, but it is not the Rock of Gibraltar. It is a note in the scale, but not the entire scale and certainly not the complete song.

Who, for example, thinks of sex when he sees a hockey player go streaking down the ice, weaving around the defense, and rifling a winning shot? Who thinks of sex when pondering the terms of a mortgage, or prowling for a bargain in the supermarket, or waiting anxiously in a dentist's office?

The trouble is that the world and the devil unite to overemphasize the flesh through magazines that might just as well be mud sandwiches, through paperbacks that crawl like cans of worms, through plays and novels that could have been spewed out of a sewer, through seductive dress or rather undress — all this exaggerates the normal sex drive into a savage, primitive, raw, rushing whirl.

Secondly, if sex is only a part of human life, and not

the whole picture, it must (to be true to humanity) run along the car tracks of human (and not animal) nature. Some years ago a denominational welfare council published a booklet that said, "Sex is the ground of all social life, because it is the basic human fact." Not at all. Sex may be *a* basic human fact, but it is not *the* basic human fact. If sex were *the* basic human fact, it would be what distinguishes human beings from all other beings. But obviously animals have sex, and in a certain sense even flowers have sex. What distinguishes us from the birds and the bees and the bisons is not sex, which we share with them, but a human soul which is ours alone.

That human soul is the seat of our intelligence, the source of our reasoning (which animals do not have), the fountain of our art, literature, music (ever see an animal opera house?), the origin of our courts, our highways, our machines, our cathedrals. The faculty of sex is set in the whole man, and cannot be truly exercised independent of human mind and heart. Animals can mate, satisfy passion, and casually trot away after a merely physical encounter, but man cannot really isolate sex from his complete human nature.

That is why we cannot say, "God gave me a sexual appetite, so why not go ahead and indulge it?" We have to say, "God gave me a sexual appetite as part of my human nature and therefore I must restrict it within human bounds, which means, subject to conscience, conscious of the commandments, and aware of the rights of my fellow-men."

Of course if a man does not believe in God or in eternity or in a last judgment, there is no clear reason for him to be moral in the realm of sex, or, for that matter, in any other department of life. If he really is convinced that the black curtain of death spells an end to the human play, if it all winds up as a Thanksgiving dinner for some hungry worms, or as a super-ash-tray in a crematorium, and that is *finis,* with nothing, absolutely nothing afterwards, then why not get away with all he can, taking care of course not to be caught?

The good of your fellow-man? If God is not the Father of you both, then your neighbor need be no more to you than an ibis in Africa. Be good to those people you like, and perish the rest! The welfare of society? Take what you can from society, and give as little as you must. Let the simpletons push society's cart, while the sophisticates ride!

After all, you are here for only a number of years, and if (presumably) you are not going to get caught, and if there is nothing after this, then why not rob and rape, seduce and defile, perjure and embezzle, break hearts, break promises, break commandments, and take your neighbor's wallet or his wife?

Does all this seem outrageous, revolting, sickening? Certainly it does, because the fact is, that there is a God, and that we are all His children, and that we know there is right and there is wrong, and whether we are detected or not, it still is right or wrong. God has wound up each man's conscience like a watch, and while we can adjust the hands to kid ourselves along, we know we are only deceiving ourselves, and we cannot stop that watch of conscience or ever really silence its ticking.

When people praise promiscuity as liberty, ask them to recall Rousseau, that arch-champion of naturalism. He had several sexual alliances, but something decent inside prompted him to turn over his five illegitimate children to the orphanage of the Sisters of Charity. This is the man who branded religion as slavery, but he still wanted to make sure that those helpless infants would be fed and clothed and not left in a Paris gutter to turn blue with cold or to be torn by roaming dogs. Notice how he held on to the devil with one hand, but with the other he held tightly to the Church and civilization. He did not really want to go back to "nature."

Thirdly, we must realize that man's sex is 1) only a part of life, and 2) a part of strictly human nature that ever since the fall of man, 3) has been *wounded* and scarred, tilted toward evil, so that the will is weak and the passions strong. To be what we should be, we need outside help, that is, the grace of God. Unless that grace of God sit, as it were, like the engineer in the cab, our passions will roar away with us like a runaway locomotive. We cannot be good unless God give it, but God *will* give it, unfailingly, if we ask. The saints have found it is easiest to ask through her who was Virgin and Mother, the Morning Star, unsmudged by any grime of earth. She can change, even a stable into a cathedral, as at Bethlehem once she really did.

A Prod from God

Now and then some research organization completes a national survey, takes off its horn-rimmed spectacles, tilts its publicity microphone and triumphantly announces that it has just discovered what nobody in his sane senses had ever doubted.

One such project recently probed the subject of happiness and revealed first, that girls are happiest if they can marry in their twenties. This is a revelation? Secondly, that most men will be happiest at their job if they are doing the kind of work they like. Who would want to take the negative on that? Thirdly, that the happiest married couples are those who find recreation and entertainment at home rather than on the gaudy merry-go-round of outside amusements. Fourthly, that the finances of the family have nothing essentially to do with its happiness, except that the very poor would surely be happier if they had more, and the very rich would probably be happier if they had less. The fifth and final conclusion was that the best way for any of us to be happy is to be glad for what we have and not to pine after what we have not.

The trouble is that most of us almost unconsciously demand an uninterrupted procession of happiness and are indignant when one of the floats in the parade breaks down. I can imagine such a sad-sack sniffling and snuffling and complaining of his troubles, when suddenly a saint appears, in traditional white robe and bright halo. As the complainer goes whining on, the saint quietly removes his golden halo, polishes it thoughtfully with a silk handkerchief, and gently asks, "Did it ever occur to you that you are not supposed to be happy all the time on this sinful old earth?"

The truth is, of course, that we are not. This world is only the exam room in which we take our tests for graduating into heaven. It is not vacation time, not the grand prize. It is the road, not the goal. It is the weary work, not the welcome rest. The catechism warned us about this on its very first page, but we were too young to understand. Remember how it said that God made us to know Him, to love Him, to serve Him in this life, and to be happy with Him in the next? *In the next.* Duty now, perfect happiness later.

Sometimes, when our cherished plans go crashing off the track it may help to remember that this is not a perfect world, and that God never meant it as such. As yet we are only apprentice angels, journeymen saints, with no right to complete happiness. Look at life this way and you will see any sudden, surprising piece of happiness as an unexpected and undeserved bonus. This is not to say that we cannot be the architects of our own relative personal happiness. To a great extent we can, if we do two things. First, stay in the state of grace (that is, the friendship of God) by a good life. To attempt to have any true happiness and have at the same time a bad conscience is like trying to smile with your front teeth while there is a throbbing abscess in the back.

The second step is to appreciate the good fortune that we do have, that is, our blessings. Part of this means recognizing that, in the old phrase, most of our troubles are little ones. How many major disasters could a man survive? It is the minor ones that keep leaving their irritations on our doorstep, as regularly as the morning paper. It is the small vexations that keep the flag of our disposition at half-staff. It is not the awesome charge of trumpeting elephants overwhelming us with a great tragedy, but it is the piercing whine and the spiteful stab of life's little mosquitoes that get us down.

We miss a bus, or we lose a filling, or we get a flat tire, or we mislay the car keys, or we spill a red sea of catsup over a snowy linen tablecloth, and we wonder why these exasperating things have to happen. Do we ever think that God may be trying to get our attention? It has been said so well that God is like the doctor — we think of Him only when we are in trouble. When the lake is a serene stretch of dimpled blue, who ever thinks of prayer? When the sky grows tarry black, and the lightning hurls its white harpoons, and the waves rear up like frothing monsters, then the prayers begin. Then we think of God.

This could hold in minor troubles too. Suppose the dryer breaks down at the moment fresh clothes are an imperative. It can make you lose your temper, but it can also help you find God. It can remind you that on this vast earth many things happen over which we have no control. From that it is an easy step to the Creator of the earth, the author of all natural laws, even down to the pressure and strain of a cog in a machine. It makes you mentally glance up to headquarters. Prosperity goes its whistling way forgetful of God, but adversity digs you in the ribs and nudges you to remember Him. Trouble is often a prod from God.

For example, I had spent a couple of hours martialing the thoughts for this chapter on the uses of adversity. When I had the notes lined up and arranged logically for transcription on the typewriter, I put them aside. At least I thought so. Later I went to look for them. They had completely disappeared. Nobody took them (that would have been a crime without a motive) — they fell out of a pocket or were mistakenly thrown into a wastebasket or maybe were left in a dentist's waiting room. At any rate, they disappeared. So I thought to myself, here is exactly what I was writing about. If something turns against you, let it turn you to God. So I said a little prayer of resignation that I never would have said — a "Thy will be done, O Lord" — that otherwise would never have been thought of. After I had thus briefly talked to God, He seemed to talk to me. He said — the essay wasn't so good anyway.

Now and then, I suppose, God has to use some device, even like tripping us up to get our attention. Otherwise, how seldom we think of God in the rush and bustle of life! Rarely we even nod in the direction of Him from whom we all come, on whom we all ultimately depend! It is a wise man who uses a sudden mishap to put him in communication with heaven. He turns trouble inside out and finds that on the other side is written the autograph of God.

In large hospitals, doctors carry gadgets clipped to their pockets that buzz or beep when they are wanted. In the same way little setbacks can be sharp, shrill reminders to get in touch with the Lord for the patience and the courage and the strength we need in this very imperfect world.

Naturally, we should like to be free of all annoyances, all these pebbles in the comfortable shoes of placid life. Who could not get along without poison ivy, frozen pipes, ball-points that suddenly go dry, sprained ankles, and dreary rain on a summer picnic? On the other hand without these, might not life become so serene it would grow stagnant, like a stream that has slowed down from ripples to scum? Maybe we would become like the mother who, on a schoolday morning when there is a mad rush for books and lunches or raincoats or mislaid mittens, yearns for peace and quiet. Before she knows it, the children are grown up and moved out, and everything is silent and dignified and civilized, only now that she has her peace and quiet she secretly wishes there was a little noise and confusion and life.

Whether we want it or not, life's little vexations, irritations, frustrations are going to be present, and each ought to be treated as a tiny light flashing on the switch-board to put us in brief, prayerful contact with God. Let that particular ill-wind swing us around like a weather vane toward Him and heaven.

Instead of a burst of profanity, try a little prayer, a sort of smiling "Dear Lord, this is rough, but I guess you know what's best." It won't help you catch the missed train or put together the broken vase, but it will help sweeten a sour situation. It will even sanctify what might have been some degree of sin. In fact, a certain French writer, whose name I cannot now recall and could never easily pronounce, praises such resignation in adversity as "the Sacrament of the present moment."

God sent angels to the shepherds and a star to the Three Kings. When he wants to get *our* attention He sometimes sends trouble. Maybe if we thought of Him and turned to Him more often of our own accord, He would not have to tap us on the shoulder with some little trial or jostle us with some jolting disappointment. But if it does come, treat it as a prod from God.

LOAVES AND FISHES

Sermons in Stones

For many decades Roxbury, Ma., (where this is written) has been a part of Boston. When it walked alone as a separate town it had its own seal and motto: "Saxetum Deo et dextris confidens!" Roughly it translates into: "This rocky place relies on God and its own right arm!"

Rocky is the word. The rectory window looks out on a huge shoulder of a flint ledge. The twin-spired basilica next door was built of Roxbury pudding stone which was quarried hardly a stone's throw from its site. This Mission Church (as it was called in the beginning and is still called now) rises like a fortress whose walls glint like granite that has turned honey color after soaking up a century of sun. A wooden church may be more homey and devotional; a brick church may be neater; a concrete church may be cheaper, but for strength and majesty, give me a church of rugged stone.

Many years ago I saw a church in Pittsburgh, Pa., where the whole inner wall of the sanctuary was studded with famous stones. To the best of my memory it was Calvary Episcopal Church, and I found myself there not in anticipation of our present ecumenical camaraderie, but because I missed my real target which was the nearby Catholic church of the Sacred Heart.

However, once inside, like a comparison shopper in

the establishment of a competitor, I launched on a pious prowl and was startled and delighted to come upon a sanctuary wall set with exotic stones, each identified by a plaque. One stone had come from the ancient Temple of Jerusalem, another from Mount Olivet, and there was even a group of five small polished stones from the brook where David picked his ammunition when he whirled his sling and grounded Goliath. The other stones I do not recall, except one that was neatly embedded far to the right with a sort of left-handed inscription: "From Armagh, where Patrick the Briton brought Christianity to the Irish." True perhaps, but you could get stones thrown at you in Boston for emphasizing it.

As a Catholic I naturally felt that this varied collection was without the most important stone of all, the Rock of Peter, the papacy, the great solid stone on which Christ had built His Church. So I sauntered across the street to the Catholic church that had been my original destination, and although it had no such assortment of historical fragments, I found myself thinking of the occasions when stones had their brief dramatic moments in the life of our Lord.

The marble altar of the Mass, for example, brought to mind that scene in the wilderness when the devil had pointed to the round stones that were shaped like loaves of bread, and had scornfully said, "If you *are* the Son of God, command that these stones be changed into bread." The thought came now, with a little gasp of gratitude, that Christ has done even better than that, for every day on this altar stone He changes bread into His own Body. How casually we take the incredible for granted!

Then my eye wandered down the side wall of the church. The stone was as rough on the inside as you might expect to find it on the outside. At regular intervals along this rugged inside wall, confessionals jutted out like wayside shrines. Out of curiosity, I looked into one and saw the little screen. Suddenly it was like television. I seemed to see, in imagination's own rich color, a little group of hard-faced men muttering threats in their beards as they pushed a disheveled woman before them. They gave her one final, brutal shove and she fell sprawling and crying in the dust of the crossroad. Meanwhile you could hear their shouts: "Adulteress! Law of Moses! The penalty is death!" And they were gathering stones.

The terrified woman pushed aside her long hair. There was Jesus, seated on a rock, His large eyes looking at her with melting pity. He scanned her accusers with eyes out of which leaped lightnings, and said, "Let him who is without sin cast the first stone!" Then He stooped low and began to write in the dust. No play ever had a curtain like this, as one by one they stared over His shoulder, read the tracings on the sand, dropped a stone, and slunk away in silent shame.

Jesus Christ still sits, by His delegated power, in every confessional. "Whose sins you shall forgive, they are forgiven." How often a hypocritical world, after using its victim, pharisaically flings her away as unclean and disgraced!

In the confessional, she can find grace once more in the understanding pardon of God. Any man, when he feels his conscience pursuing him along the road of the past, flinging his old sins after him like dirty stones, when he feels himself beaten down under a pounding onslaught of black and bitter memories, can come to Christ in the Sacrament and find protection, can bury his past and come forth risen. He has only to promise that he will try his level best to chart his future course by the words of Jesus to that woman: "Go and sin no more!"

It is no exaggeration to say that the life of our Lord could be portrayed as a huge mosaic made up of rocks and stones. He was born in a cave hollowed out of a rocky hill at Bethlehem. He was buried in a tomb that was sealed with a great stone at Calvary. At His first miracle He commanded the water pots of stone to be filled before He changed their brimming content, like pools at sunset, into crimson wine. In His harshest moment of anger, He boomed: "It would be better for that man that a millstone be tied round his neck and he be drowned in the depths of the sea."

He had pity for the seed that fell upon stony ground. He had praise for the prudent man who built his house not upon shifting sands but upon a solid rock. He had a dire forboding about Jerusalem which, He said, would be destroyed so that there would not be a stone left upon a stone. He referred to Himself as the stone which the builders rejected, but which became indeed the cornerstone of the edifice. He had even acted to save His own life (for Calvary was not yet due) by disappearing into thin air as the crowd took up stones to kill Him.

Shakespeare said there are sermons in stones, and there probably are, if we have the fresh eye to find them. St. Stephen, the first Christian martyr was stoned to death, crumpling under a shower of rocks that spurted from the fire-hot volcano of a mob's anger. Conversely, St. Alphonsus Liguori, while writing his moral theology, would press a cold stone to his hot and throbbing temples. St. Jerome, at prayer in his hermit's cave, but haunted and taunted by the lurid memories of his youth in the city, would snatch up a stone and beat his breast as if to pound the temptation to powder. St. John Nepomucene, when he refused to reveal the queen's confession to the king, was trussed up in a canvas sack that was weighted down with rocks and tossed into the icy river.

For the average Christian, the end is not so grim, but when it does come, when the last milestone has been passed, there remains for each of us the headstone. Should not that very word, headstone, suggest that it marks a beginning rather than an end? "Requiescat in Pace," is a forwarding address to a land so happy and rich that even the jewels of this old earth, its so-called precious stones, will seem like drab and shoddy pebbles. "Eye hath not seen nor ear heard," promises St. Paul, "what God hath prepared for those that love Him." To the believer, each day is only a stepping-stone toward Heaven.

The Big Ten

In these amiable days of ecumenism when there is so much emphasis on *dialogue* (a Greek word for friendly communication with our non-Catholic neighbors) there may be some danger of underplaying the *decalogue* (a Greek word for the original and basic Ten Commandments).

Contrary to a conviction current in some motion picture production circles, the Ten Commandments did not originate with Cecil B. DeMille, though he did use them in one of his run-of-de-mill epics. I get the impression that the result was another case of many a slip between the Scripture and the script.

Some people are pained by pictures about the Ten Commandments; others are puzzled by sculptures symbolizing the Ten Commandments. Everybody knows that while smoke billowed above sacred Mount Sinai, and while the thunder rumbled its kettle-drums, and the lightning shook its white spears — Moses came down from an awesome audience with God carrying two gray slabs on which were written the Ten Commandments. Carvings representing these tablets in glistening marble adorn many Catholic pulpits. What puzzles the normal layman with a sense of symmetry is why there should be three numerals or commandments on one tablet and seven on the other, instead of a nicely balanced five on each.

The reason generally offered is that the first three commandments refer to our obligations toward God, while the other seven relate to our obligations toward our neighbor. However, if you saw a Protestant pulpit, you would probably find the tablets divided into four commandments and six commandments. In fact, if you were discussing stealing with a Protestant friend, and casually mentioned the Seventh Commandment, he might very well interject: "Oh, no! The Seventh Commandment forbids adultery." His minister in all probability would back him up too.

It turns out then that there are two different enumerations of the commandments. The Catholics and the Lutherans follow an order that goes back to St. Augustine. Most other Protestants and the Orthodox follow another listing dating back to Origen. The confusion arises because in early Hebrew there were no paragraphs; in fact there were not even vowels, only vowel points. It was hard, therefore, to tell where one commandment ended and where the next began. You might even surmise at first reading that there were eleven commandments; this is the nub of the difficulty.

The Catholic Church combines the *first* two precepts into one commandment, reasoning that it is all under the general prohibition of false worship. The Protestants combine the *last* two precepts into one commandment, maintaining that this all comes under the broad umbrella of coveting, whether it is coveting one's neighbor's wife or his goods. In this way, both of them harmoniously add up to ten, though there is confusion in the middle. A mere matter of semantics, my dear Watson.

When you think of all the libraries of law books, it is amazing how wide a span this simple rainbow of the Ten Commandments arches. Family rights, property rights, the rights of God and the rights of the individual are all included. Sparse and clean-cut, the Ten Command-

ments are like the slender steel scaffolding of the whole
cathedral of morality. Now and then, of course, some
glib liberal, who has been educated beyond his intelligence, solemnly pontificates from his professorial
podium that the music needs a new arrangement. He
dismisses the Ten Commandments as being as outmod-
ed as Prohibition. He insists that a new world needs a
new ethic. He wants to know why modern men should be
burdened with the primitive code of a nomadic tribe
which lived under skin tents in an ancient desert.

The tents or the tribe or the desert we do not dis-
pute. But it is an amazing truth that if you change the
tents to ranch houses or split-levels or elevator apart-
ments; if you change the desert to downtown in any big
city or to the suburbs beyond; if you change the nomadic
tribe to traveling executives in business suits with brief-
cases — it is monumentally true that old human nature
is still what it always was. Things have changed. The
scratching stylus has become the electric typewriter.
The clicking abacus has become the whirring computer.
The creaking ox-cart has become the jet. But fire is still
fire, water is still water, and man is still man. He has the
same temptations, the same passions, the same weak-
nesses, the same pitfalls as ever.

That is why, aside from the purpose of emphasis
and with one partial exception, the Ten Commandments need never have been promulgated on Mount
Sinai at all. Long before God gave Moses the Ten Commandments written on tablets of stone, He had engraved
them on the fleshy tablet of the human heart. They were
inside us, almost like instincts. Who was not aware in his
secret soul that he should worship his Maker? Who did
not know that a child should obey his parents? Who ever
doubted that it was wrong to lie or steal or murder or
commit adultery?

The Ten Commandments were only like the em-
bossed numerals on the dial of everyman's conscience,
and when he violated any of them that conscience rang
like an alarm. Centuries before Moses, these command-

ments bound Adam and Eve and their children in and beyond the Garden of Paradise; and centuries after Moses, they bound the Apostles in the Garden of Gethsemane. They were not made for any particular period in history. They were based on human nature and therefore were commandments for all seasons, for all centuries, as universal and perpetual as honor or truth.

You may be curious as to the exceptions alluded to above. Well, man knew in general that he had an obligation to worship God, but it took the Third Commandment to pinpoint one special day of the week and set it apart for that divine worship. In the old Law, the realm of patriarchs and prophets, of Temple and Torah, of bearded highpriests and smoking sacrifices, this day was the seventh day of the week. On that day, in the story of Creation, God had rested. In fact *Sabbath,* as the seventh day was called, means in Hebrew rest or repose.

But, at the coming of Christ, the book of the Old Testament was closed like the clap of thunder on Calvary. Its wisdom endured but its ritual was ended. Now, on the lectern in the sanctuary of Christianity, the book of the New Testament was opened. Henceforth new rites would prevail. Christians, standing at the empty tomb of Christ and seeing in His tombstone the cornerstone of the new Church, now chose Sunday, the day on which He rose, as the day that hereafter would be sacred to the Lord. Traditionally Sunday was also the day on which the Church was born when the Holy Spirit descended upon the Apostles at Pentecost. Furthermore, this changing of the day of worship from Saturday to Sunday was a vivid way of saying that Moses and the whole Jewish religion had been, like John the Baptist, only a forerunner of Christ, and now that Christ was come, the synagogue should gracefully slip back into spiritual retirement.

Jews do not believe this, of course, and we respect their convictions. Seventh Day Adventists also keep the Sabbath, and we honor them not least of all for their logic. It is difficult to see how the people who proclaim that they take their religion from the Bible and the Bible alone, can reconcile their observance of Sunday as the Lord's Day. You can go through the New Testament with the finest of fine combs and not come out with one verse that justifies the changing of the Sabbath from Saturday to Sunday. Catholics take their beliefs from both Scripture *and* Tradition. Each is basically the truth of God, the one written, the other handed down orally from generation to generation. In this particular instance, it is only Tradition that tells us plainly that the infant Church, conscious that she was the echo of a divine voice ("He who hears you, hears Me") buried the Sabbath with Christ and chose the day of His Resurrection, Sunday, as the Lord's Day.

But it was not just by choosing a new day (Sunday) and keeping it in a new way (Holy Mass) that made early Christianity spread like a spark running through a field of dry stubble in that wondrous prairie fire of the early faith. It was not just keeping the Third Commandment but all the Commandments. It was not only miracles, though they were there, but the eye-opening marvel of men and women living decent and charitable lives in the midst of a paganism that was a blend of faded scarlet pride and iron cruelty, and nauseating, muddy immorality. It was from the soil of *keeping God's law* that Christianity flowered.

Should not the badge of the Christian be the same today? Booming down the arches of the centuries, the voice of Christ rings as clearly as ever at our own doorstep: "If you love Me, keep My commandments." His commandments were The Commandments, which He even capsulized into the two great commandments of love of God and love of neighbor. He did not say: If you love Me, move to the suburbs." Nor, "If you love Me, enroll in college." Nor, "If you love Me, dress with fashionable elegance." Nor, "If you love Me, make your pile early." He offered only one test — "If you love Me, keep the Commandments." Other things, good, bad, or indifferent, might merely prove that we loved ourselves.

If a pastor asked a group of his people: "Do you love God?", everybody would answer "Yes," and nobody would say "No." But does a doctor ask a patient: "What is your blood-pressure?" Hardly. He has a special instrument by which he can be sure. Each of us, too, has an infallible instrument to measure our love of Jesus Christ, our God. He gave it to us Himself. Do we keep the Commandments? It is that simple.

When Moses came down from the smoking mountain, he carried two tablets of stone, the hard symbol of God's stern justice. When Mary came forth from the stable of Bethlehem, she bore in her arms the tiny Christ Child, the soft symbol of God's mercy. Through her who is full of grace, may we all get that double grace we so desperately need — forgiveness for Commandments broken in the past, and fidelity to keep the Commandments in the years, few or many, that lie ahead.

Those Sunday Collections

On a recent February afternoon I was invited to preach, in tune with the new ecumenical tempo, in a Methodist church. Fearful perhaps that I might launch into some peppery theme like "Papal Infallibility," the priest heading the committee suggested I take as my theme "The Spirit of Lent," which presumably was neutral ground. The talk was probably as vague as its title, but if it bored the congregation, the service certainly did not bore me. I was both fascinated and yet ill at ease.

The stately procession, the robed chancel choir, the sonorous reading of favorite psalms, the personal, extemporaneous prayer by the minister — all these impressed me deeply but left me vaguely uncomfortable.

Then the minister ascended the pulpit again, and in his rich, resonant voice announced, "We shall now take up the collection." At once I began to feel at home. Shortly before, he had leaned over and whispered, "We Methodists may not sing sweet, but we do sing loud." By way of contrast, that Methodist collection was strangely quiet. Are we Catholics, I wondered, different in this, that our singing is weak and faltering, while our collections jangle? On reflection I doubt it.

We are not a wealthy group, but look at what we

have produced. You have only to survey the vast fleet of Catholic steeples and the regiments of parochial schools dotting our country, and you realize that American Catholics have been very generous to the Church, perhaps more generous than any other nation in history. But then are we not more prosperous, and our standard of living higher than any nation before us?

But please to regard (as they say on the Continent) the situation from another viewpoint. If you compare what we spend on cosmetics with what we give to Christ, or what we pay for grog with what we offer to God, or even what Protestants and Jews drop into their collection baskets in proportion to what we put into ours, then our munificence melts and our pride in giving must take on a slow blush. We do not really give what we could, or what we should.

Vatican II left the door wide open for this, even if it was a side door. One of the prime purposes of the Council was to encourage a more mature Catholicity. To this end the laws of fasting and abstinence were adjusted in the hope that we would do some fasting and abstaining and other sacrificing on our own. In a way this is much harder, because there is no regiment with which to keep step. However, one form of sacrifice is always available: almsgiving, which is the Sunday-suit term for personal contact with the collection plate. And is there any better object of our sacrifices than our parish church? Or is there any cause that needs it more?

Pity, then, the poor, debt-harried pastor who wishes that the good Lord had given him a fiery eloquence that would melt the metal clasps on any reluctant purse, and warm the icy heart that beats so coldly beneath the indifferent wallet. Instead he is forced to mumble some vapid cliché, some ancient retread like "Please be as generous as your means will allow." He is well aware that he is not by nature nor grace a salesman but only a soulsman, and asking for money is a task he cordially hates.

If there were only some rhetorical novocaine that

would make the financial extraction painless! But how should he go about it? Tell his parishioners that they are the salt of the earth, and then proceed to shake them down? Call them the cream of the diocese, and then skim off the top? No matter what his approach, he will always yearn for that distant day when, just as there is in the year only one Ash Wednesday, there will also be only one Cash Sunday. Then, for the rest of the weeks and months he could forget about the dollar-sign and concentrate on the sign of the cross.

There are, it is said, one or the other non-Catholic churches where a few affluent members flourish a philanthropic pen across an annual check so that these signatures of the mighty literally underwrite the parish budget. With the average Catholic congregation it is quite the contrary.

The ordinary Catholic church is held up somewhat in the style of the George Washington Bridge. What you see there are four gracefully dipping cables, but you are really looking at only cable coverings. Inside are hundreds upon hundreds of tiny wires, intertwined and interwoven; and all these, insignificant alone but mighty together, divide the burden and support the bridge. In similar fashion Catholics must always depend not on a few who are wealthy but on many who are willing. In New York City it has always been an adage that St. Patrick's Cathedral was built in all its monumental majesty by the regular small contributions of Irish servant-girls.

These latter days, too, parish collections are feeling the impact of another phenomenon. We used to be Roman Catholics. Now, with the multiplication of the motor-car we have become Roamin' Catholics. The nearest church is not necessarily the most convenient church. One church has a broader schedule of Masses, another has a gifted preacher, a third one has no steps to climb ("completely on the level" is the winking description) while still another is right on the way to the beach; not forgetting the one a quarter mile down whose pastor is called, "In again, out again, gone again, Finnegan," because you are always sure of a fast track and a short session.

Thus people casually select the church where they will hear Mass on a particular Sunday. BUT (and the letters should be tall as telephone poles) wherever we go, we still have an obligation to support our own parish church. That once-a-year check to the church, and no Sunday collections, at all, would solve everything, wouldn't it? And that is just the way they run things at St. Nemo's, Utopia.

Meanwhile, however, the Offertory is part of the liturgy and the collection is its prosaic adjunct, even though the present designation is presentation of the gifts. Come to think of it, even before there is a parish church, money is necessary to build one. That is where *u* and *i* come in, in build. But at least a new church is something you can see and appreciate. In most parishes, though, it is not a matter of building a church, but a question of maintaining what a preceding generation has built.

We are all human, and we like our money to show. It is very much like the memorial situation. Let a pastor in a reasonably large city parish (I mean one that is still dynamic and thriving, not an ecclesiastical fossil) appeal during the Sunday Masses for a dozen new vestments, each to be donated in memory of some deceased relative and to be duly inscribed or even embroidered. The generous response will usually whip back fast as an echo, and the request may easily be oversubscribed.

But, if the ceiling in the crying-room is peeling, do you think many people will be eager to give 50 square yards of anonymous plaster, even though it might serve as a likely memorial for poor Uncle Bill, who was known to have been on occasion plastered himself?

The thought of plaster, gently trapezes to the thought of paint. In some parishes people who did not have too much money (who has?) but who did have interest of their parish at heart, have gotten together to paint the parish hall or the school classrooms. The work was done in the evenings and over the week-ends, generally on a co-ed basis.

The men manned the rollers and the women varnished the sills and prepared the sandwiches and coffee. Such a project obviously cuts down on parish expenses but also notably builds up parish pride. ("After all, Michelangelo's best job was a ceiling, wasn't it?") Buckets and mops, rollers and paint, plus a congenial crowd make for unity and solidarity that was not there before, like a sprinkling of freckles uniting into a coat of tan. More than once it has happened that when the last paint brush was rinsed and the job was done, the workers were sorry to return to the monotony of idle evenings with TV repeats.

Even where we give time and talent, there must also be the weekly confrontation with the collection basket. The priest may pass out the envelopes and pray for many happy returns. He may point out that the bazaar will take off your clean hands all those old, grimy, germ-ridden dollar bills. He may subtly refer to road signs that plead, "Keep Cape Cod Green!" But in the congregation the response will ring up "No Sale" unless as individuals they are convinced that since this is their church, and not the pastor's, it is their duty to do what they can toward supporting it. In the end we put our money where our faith is.

I once heard a foreign missionary say, very quietly and evenly, to the crowded pews: "I am not asking you for what you can afford. When I think of the high price of food, and clothing, and education for your children, of rent and mortgages and taxes, I realize that if I were to take back with me what you can afford, I would take back nothing. I am asking what you cannot afford. I am asking what you must sacrifice. I am asking for God."

The same is true, even more so, when it comes to something so close to us as our own parish church. We are giving not what we can easily afford, but what we can hardly afford.

That is why it helps to remember that when we die,

we carry off in our clutched hands only what we have given away.

You can't take it with you. You can send it ahead. The usher is holding the basket, but you are putting your offering into the wounded palm of Christ.

The Globe Is a Prayerbook
(Spirituality for the Space Age)

You must have heard of the little girl who was breaking in her new set of crayons. Her mother looked across from the ironing-board and asked, "What are you drawing, dear?" The little girl answered, "I'm drawing a picture of God." "But," said the mother, "nobody knows what God looks like." The child answered simply, "Now they will."

It is impossible to get an autographed photograph of God; it is hard to get an idea of Him. If you want to go insane in a pleasant sort of way, try pouring into the midget computer of your brain all the data about God; His all-seeing knowledge, His infinite power, His incomprehensible greatness and majesty. Start with where you live, somewhere in the suburbs of space. In the postal system of the universe, with its whirling suns and stars and moons and planets, our address is the earth. This earth with its huge continents and vast oceans, its towering mountains and its teeming cities, is in our human view certainly not small. There are stars in the calm evening sky that make the earth look as insignificant as the little black period at the end of a sentence.

For instance in the constellation Orion there is a star with the weird name of Betelgeuse. Long ago in the seminary where we had a tall observatory that looked like a giant salt-shaker with a revolving roof, that "beetle-juice" was always good for a laugh. But the size of it made you frown. If this earth is twenty-five-thousand miles in circumference and the average man were six feet (he isn't of course; people like me drag the average down) Betelgeuse is so large that the average man, to be in proportion, would have to be forty five miles high.

Dull red Antares glows in the sky no bigger that a strawberry but it would take sixty thousand earths to equal it. It is like comparing a caraway seed to a watermelon. There are many stars so far away that one of our space capsules rocketing along at seventeen thousand miles an hour would not reach them for seventeen thousand years. In fact some stars are so remote that the ray of light that left them the day Christ was born has not reached us yet, though it has been travelling one hundred and eighty six thousand miles a second.

Who can cram so awesome a picture on the twelve-inch TV screen of his human mind? And yet so much greater is the Creator God than any of His creations, that to Him these immense and immeasurable stellar bodies appear only like clusters of white grapes trailing across the vine of the midnight sky.

Put down the telescope and take up the microscope. Think of a fluttery wisp of a moth in some unexplored South American jungle. No man has ever seen that creature and no man ever will. God sees every twitch of its slender antennae. When it brushes past a bush He sees every particle of powdery dust that filters down from its left wing. Perhaps at that very moment on the other side of the world a mountainous wave booms against the Australian coast and splinters into silvery spray. God knows where every separate drop falls into the great anonymous ocean. Or pick out one snowflake in a howling Siberian blizzard. Millions of other flakes are falling around it, before it, after it, but God has blueprinted every inch of *this* flake's nervous, dipping, swirling path. How crude the image if we compare Him to the Master

Engineer sitting at the controls of the universe! How can we picture Him at all?

For that matter, how did it all start, this tremendous universe or even our own little earth? All we have are some thin theories, heavily padded with possibilities, and dressed in long triple-jointed words. It does not much matter, because every new trail that is cut up the mountainside of scientific investigation eventually has to lead to the ultimate peak which is God. About half a century ago we were taught that once upon a time (a fine beginning for a fairy tale) a truant star whizzed closely past the sun. Its gravity pulled at the sun's edge, and a chip snapped off the sun and went whistling away on a blazing track of its own, a new speedster in space. We were then assured that this fragment of fiery gases cooled for millions of years in the deep-freeze of time, and finally emerged cooled off and tolerably comfortable to become our earth. It is quite a wild diary for a little orphan planet, but once it did have a very popular sale.

The trouble with any such explanation, even if it were true, is that it does not go back far enough. It does not go back to the beginning. Once you mention a whirling sun, or a star that ran outside its base-line, the mind automatically asks who started that sun whirling, and where did the errant star come from? In matters of this kind we are interested only in first editions. In fact we are curious above all about the Author. After all, if out of nothing (no matter how long you wait) there comes only nothing, and here and now there is something, then there always must have been something.

More than something. Someone. We call a certain portion of the heavens the solar system, because it is a system, and a system implies a Mind. The stars are not spinning around aimlessly like colored marbles in a tray. We can set our watches by their precision.

We can predict eclipses fifty years in advance and to the minute, so accurate are celestial orbits. It follows then that we must either admit behind all this a deliberate plan, or be prepared to accept a colossal coincidence.

A. Cressy Morrison, a former president of the New York Academy of Sciences, once drew up a long list of lucky breaks this little earth had; only he couldn't see how any logician could make the list add up to mere luck. For example our globe rotates on its axis at a speed of about a thousand miles an hour. If it revolved only a hundred miles an hour, then the long, long hot day would shrivel all vegetation. That axis is tilted at an angle of about twenty three degrees. If it were not, every continent would be a giant lifeless glacier. The earth is about two hundred and forty thousand miles from the moon. If it were only forty thousand miles away, the tides would be so enormous that twice a day every country would be completely under water. The atmosphere around the earth is heavy enough to protect it like an envelope or an umbrella. If it were thinner, meteors would be falling upon us in constant showers like incendiary bombs. Quite a procession of lucky situations!

Ask the average American if he believes in God and he answers, "Sure, I believe in God." Ask him why, and although he may speak in groping, stumbling words, his meaning is as simple as bread and as solid as stone. The common man sees the great green garden of each new spring and knows that behind it there must be a gardener. He sees the starry blueprint of the evening sky and he knows that behind it there must be a draftsman. He sees so fragile a motor as the whir of a hummingbird's wings, so delicate a camera as the incredible human eye, so huge a heart-beat as the regular rising and falling of the tide, and the common man's common sense tells him that behind the product is the Producer, the Designer, the Master Craftsman. Only if he saw a load of bricks that had just been dumped on a streetcorner, form themselves into a house; or if he saw a pile of tiny wheels and springs tossed on a desk arrange themselves into a smooth-running watch, only then might he believe that a world (incidentally more wonderful than any house and more complicated than any watch) could make itself, without benefit of a Maker.

The real danger is that the average man is likely to downgrade his own importance when confronted with the magnitude of the universe. He lifts his eyes to the vastness of space and the overwhelming grandeur of gigantic suns and stars, and wonders, "What can I, one insignificant man, matter in the presence of all this?" The answer is that you matter precisely because you are a man, and therefore can never be insignificant.

Certainly you are small when compared with the earth or the cosmos. For that matter you are small when compared with an elephant or a ton of coal. Granted that other things occupy more space, have more tonnage, loom larger to the eye, but does this whittle away one sliver from your incomparable dignity as a human being? Does it minimize your intelligence, your ideals, your emotions, your soul? The botanist is still greater than the giant redwood he walks beneath — and classifies. The mountaineer is greater than the mountain he photographs, measures, climbs, transcends.

Man is the darling of God, created in His image, and established by His decree as lord of the world. Animals are only like logs swept along in a midnight stream, driven by the overpowering current of instinct. Man is a ship with lights burning high and bright (his intelligence) and a wheel to steer by (his free will). The destiny of the tallest tree is to fall, of the strongest animal to die, of the most brilliant star to darken and disintegrate, but man's soul was made to live forever. On God's word he is immortal.

Little wonder then that the Son of God bypassed suns and stars and pressed His sacred feet upon this poor earth. Other stars proclaim His greatness, but the Star of Bethlehem came to beg our love. God did not want to be the vague Infinite, the remote Omnipotent, the Deity so dazzling that we could not bear to look. So He came down among the only creatures that could give Him the appreciation of an intelligent brain and the affection of a human heart. He even came down to die for them. He never died for an Alp. How then can man be small?

Who, Me?

The poet Robert Burns possessed a sharp and searching eye. He took this prowling eye even into his parish kirk, and while he may not have gone there often enough to wear out the benches, on one occasion when he wandered in, he saw rather than heard a very pointed sermon. You get the impression he happened to choose a seat behind a haughty and stylish lady who thought she was Miss Perfection or Mrs. Paragon.

She stared with pompous scorn at the awkward farmers who lumbered down the aisle with their clattering brogues. She frowned at the little lighthearted girls who came skipping in. In general, she looked down her tilted nose at all the revolting specimens of uncouth peasantry around her. Meanwhile, Burns, as he tells us in his precious little poem, was looking up at her, at least at her huge white hat that towered like the turret of a battleship. And there he saw on its broad brim, plain as black on white and scurrying back and forth, a very lively little louse. He and the fellow next to him winked and smiled. Meanwhile the lady kept her pose of regal disdain, unaware that she, who was so scornful of her inferiors, was now being laughed at herself.

When the poet got home, he propped a pad against his knee and pencilled the satiric poem that pleads,

"Would some Power the gift to give us, to see ourselves as others see us!"

It is a rare gift and a priceless one. How few of us have the courage to look into the clear frank mirror of conscience! Perhaps we have been pretending so long, that we would hardly recognize ourselves. King David is a fair example of that. When he saw the beauty of Bathsheba as he played Peeping Tom on his castle roof, and then burned to possess her, he had her delivered to him like a package. Her husband, Uriah, was meanwhile away with the army, fighting one of David's wars. Later when Bathsheba confided to David that she was with child by him, the King ordered that Uriah be sent to that sector of the front where the enemy was strongest, the fighting fiercest, and the casualties highest. There Uriah swiftly met his death, and immediately David took Bathsheba to himself for good — or for evil.

Probably the news got around and the people murmured, but in those days a king was just south of almighty. To cross him could be death. Then one day into his throneroom slowly walked a sad and solemn prophet of the Lord named Nathan. "Why do you come here wearing such a dark and wintry face?" asked the king. Nathan did not answer directly; instead he told a story. "Once, your majesty, there was a certain rich man who had all kinds of possessions, houses and farms and oxen and sheep and barns and lands and everything. There was also a poor man who had no possessions at all except one precious, beloved ewe lamb. And yet this rich man callously took the poor man's one ewe lamb and had it served at his own table."

"Stop!" cried King David. "I will hear no more. Such a villain is worthy of death. Who is the wretch?"

And Nathan the prophet looked right into the royal eyes and said very quietly, "Thou art that man!" And suddenly the king saw before him the golden hair of Bathsheba, and the gory ghost of Uriah, and he slumped back on his throne, staring. He was condemned by his own lips. He had committed adultery, he had compounded it with murder, and he had tried to sweep both under the rug. And here was this prophet throwing the rug back and revealing his sins. Here was Nathan holding up David's corroded heart, his smirched soul, and daring him to look, daring him to recognize himself, to see himself as others saw him: "Thou art that man!"

Give David this credit. He did not say, "Who, me?" He put off his crown, and put on sackcloth and ashes, and went into a period of penance from which emerged the immortal *Miserere* — "Have mercy upon me, O God, according to thy great mercy! My sin rises ever before me. Wash me free of evil, and make me white as snow!" Immediately a generous God put David's sin behind His back and forgave him everything. Does not God always forgive the sinner, whether he be king or beggar, if he sincerely repents?

The trouble is there are many who do not go to God to be forgiven but who plunge into pleasure or work or any distraction in order to forget. They want to pretend that it never happened. This is like a murderer who hides the body under autumn leaves, and the wind whips them away and reveals the corpse; or he hides it under the winter's snowbanks but the spring comes and melts them. The deed is still there, and a voice whispers out of the past, "Thou art that man!"

Did you ever lift your eyes to a crucifix and think, "The long brown thorns are in His brow, but that head never harbored unclean thoughts. The long black spikes are in His hands, but those fingers never were guilty of unclean touch. The long sharp spear slashed His side in a fierce red wound, but that heart never was on fire with unclean passion. Why is *He* hanging there? What has *He* done?" Did a voice never seem to come off the cross and say, "Thou art that man! He hangs, He bleeds, He suffers, He dies for thee!"

Sometimes even in minor matters we swerve from facing the truth. A friend suddenly tells us off in crackling tones, pointing out how stingy we are, or how selfish, how moody or how nosey, how positive or how suspicious, how cold-hearted or how hot-tempered. And what is our reaction? The first impulse, when someone heaves a verbal rock, is to hurl back a bigger one. But is this Christian? Is it even rational? Is it perhaps rooted in fear? Could the other party be right and the charges true? May there not be some fire where there is so much smoke? *Are* we that man, or that woman?

Possibly the accusation is a bit exaggerated. Perhaps we are not, as they imply, as nosey as a hound's snoot, always sniffing in other people's affairs. But is there not about us something of the curious, prying busy-body? Perhaps we are not, as they hint, as moody as a yo-yo, now lifted to the heights of hilarity and the next moment dropping to the depths of dejection, but, on the other hand, do we really believe that our disposition is as level as a lake? Is it not possible that when a friend has his hand on the doorknob of our disposition he isn't quite sure whether he is going to walk into a dance or a dirge? Dare to look into the looking glass of truth! It may tell you bluntly, "Thou art that man!"

One of the main purposes of religion is to recognize ourselves for what we are and to make ourselves what we ought to be. It is not sufficient simply to go to church. At the conclusion of the Sunday Mass the priest says, "The Mass is ended. Go in peace." Does that mean that our practice of religion is ended for the week too? Does it mean we then go out into the world, and leave behind for safe keeping till next week all the virtues, like honesty, humility, charity, purity, patience, and the rest?

Come to think of it, the virtues we practice in church are mostly faith and piety. All the other virtues we practice outside of church. A man in a TB sanatarium told me that when he had been well he used to go to Mass every Sunday. He had kept it up, he said, merely as a childhood custom. He went to Mass on Sunday as easily as he wore a different suit on Sunday. He never went to confession nor Communion, and when he came out of the church doors on Sunday morning, he stopped being a Catholic for the rest of the week. You couldn't tell him from his next-door neighbor who was an admitted pagan. If this "Catholic" found it profitable to cut an ethical corner in business, he cut it. If it helped him to tell a lie about an important matter, he told it. If there was a dirty book he wanted to read, he read it. His whole standard of morality was like his lounging chair: adjustable to his immediate personal comfort.

Did he ever leave Sunday Mass after an incisive sermon and hear his conscience murmur, "Thou art that man!" Not at all. He told himself that the priest up there had to say something. It was all part of the service. But now, here in the hospital, he had begun to think, to measure values, to balance time against eternity, this world against the next, the almighty dollar against Almighty God. Life often looks different from the horizontal, and in long hours of the night, gradually on his sickroom ceiling, he saw his true self, "Thou art that man!" He had the courage to admit it and he asked God's help to change it.

We all have our faults, some of them minor, some of them perhaps even grave. We also have a source of help. Help here has to mean grace, and we know who is full of grace in herself, and who is the channel of grace for us. "Dear Mary," we can plead, "because you bore Christ at Bethlehem, and stood by Him at Calvary and, won from Him His first miracle at Cana, if there is anyone in heaven who has influence with Him and can intercede for the special and particular grace I need, thou art that woman!"

We shall obtain our grace, never fear, if we sincerely ask. Then, on our part, must come action. After this will come change. And thereafter when the devil taunts us, "Thou art that man," we can even smile and admit, "I *was* that man. I am now something better."

The Challenge of Change

Although we hear much these days about "the new Church," actually it is still the same grand, majestic old one — or does that sound like proud triumphalism? Perhaps the reaction of the wry Frenchman is best. He juts out that lower lip, lifts those eloquently skeptical shoulders, and mutters, "The more she changes, the more she is the same!" And when you add it all up, the changes amount to not much more than new window displays in Macy's or Gimbel's, while the merchandise on the counters stays pretty much the same.

Those pessimists who weep salt tears into their holy water fonts, should console themselves that things are really not *that* bad. There is still one God, still the Ten Commandments (with no local amendments) still the Seven Sacraments, still the stern reality of judgment, heaven and hell, still a single ruling Pope, and an ordained priesthood, and the serene status of Mary as the Virgin Mother of God.

This chapter will make no attempt to assay, much less probe in depth, what has happened all along the ecclesiastical front since Vatican II. It is merely a sort of skimming helicopter flight over the contemporary Catholic scene to give assurance that on most avenues traffic still flows fairly smoothly, and to surmise why on others it has clogged up and bogged down.

To repeat a previous observation, the changes are incidental rather than essential. Or, put it another way: the fabric of the tablecloth is the same as ever; only some fringes have been added, and others clipped off. Under this would come the new liturgy of the Mass, that is, the vernacular, though strictly speaking even this is a return to the very old, when the vernacular was the spoken language of the Hebrews or the Greeks or the Romans who gathered around the original altar tables.

Even at that, some tight-lipped traditionalists are still fighting a stubborn rear-guard action. Not long ago I heard one of them, with much flashing of eye and pounding of fist, express what he thought of the new liturgy. "First, they wanted the Mass in English. They got it, but I don't see any SRO signs outside my parish church. It seems to me that fewer go now than before. Then they wanted to get into the act, par-tici-pation they called it. Still, many of them don't open their mouths for the prayers, and most of them never sing. And the young ones wanted their guitars. (I heard one priest who agrees with me call it the Ukelele Eucharist. That's good!) But now that they have their folk Masses, the young people aren't breaking down the church doors either. And when they get tired of this, what new gimmick do you bring on?"

I wish this Irishman could have been an Italian because then you could have whispered that wonderful word, "Pazienza! Pazienza!" First, have a little patience. Give the new liturgy a chance. And, meanwhile, remember that it all has the approbation of the Pope. Or are we better Catholics than he is?

To swing over, in our hovering helicopter, to another sector of the religious city, there seems to be a large concentration of changes in ecumenism. Not so long ago the Catholic and Anglican statements about the Eucharist rated front-page prominence, but nothing *essentially* changed from before. If anything, it was merely a change of emphasis. At the Last Supper our Lord said, "Do this in memory of Me," so the Anglicans call their communion a Memorial Service. But Catholics point out that He also said, "This is My Body . . . This is My Blood," meaning, "This is Myself," so we call it the Real Presence. The Catholic point, of course, is that the Eucharist is not *just* a memorial.

But for the conservative, ecumenism gets even more snarled farther down the avenue. When he reads of a Protestant minister or a Jewish rabbi officiating at a Catholic marriage; when he hears of his Catholic friends taking part in a Protestant wedding in major roles like best man or maid of honor; when he sees the elaborate sanctuary of his parish church enclose a simple altar-table and become as plain as a Quaker meetinghouse; when he sees priests giving Communion in long white "episcopalian" surplices and wearing long "episcopalian" stoles outside their chasubles; when he hears from the lectern a man in a gray suit struggling through the Protestant version of the old Scripture names; when he discovers that someone has apparently gone through the church calendar with a machete and slashed out the feasts of so many saints, he is inclined to start humming "when the Saints go marching out," and to do a slow Catholic burn.

He can think of a half-dozen ways in which Catholics since the Council have apparently become more Protestant, but he cannot call to mind even one way in which Protestants have become more Catholic.

Certainly in the area of ecumenism the Church has made changes, and for each of them there is its own reasonable explanation. Suffice it to say that for them all, in the general picture, the reason and the explanation has been the outstretched hand of good will to those outside the Faith. Too long the Church had appeared as a grim citadel surrounded by a forbidding moat, so the ecumenical changes have been the lowering of the drawbridge whereby the entrance is now that much more accessible.

For the loyal Catholic, however, no more explanation should be necessary than that every ecumenical change has had the sanction of His Holiness. When you follow Paul VI, you are following Peter I, and when you follow Peter, you are following Christ.

Nobody doubts that for concerned Catholics these are tortured times. The People of God, the Pilgrim Church, as it plods on toward heaven, is walking a Way of the Cross, and our particular age seems to be a halt at one of the more harrowing stations. Nobody, of course, foresaw that this would happen.

On the contrary, everybody believed that the Council would flash like a sunburst across the Christian world. There would be a bright, brave new spiritual glow everywhere, a revitalizing of zeal in the clergy, a reawakening of faith among the laity, a resurgence of vocations to the religious orders, a renewal of the convert movement with people streaming into the purified Church.

The melancholy fact is that in almost all areas the exact opposite has taken place. Certainly not *because* of the Council, but just as certainly *since* the Council. Lay the heaviest blame on the fact that (to quote the editor of the liberal *National Catholic Reporter*), "liberal theologians dominate the public prints." The wildest views get the widest audience, not because they offer what is true but what is new, and the new, of course, is the essence of news.

To encourage the reluctant old-line Catholic to accept these strange views, the cry goes up, "Remember, as a Christian you are free! Free with the freedom of the Sons of God." Curiously, the slow response is that if we are free, we would rather have our old version. Or are we free only to follow you?

Whereupon the liberal Catholic is likely to assume a patronizing and even paternal air and remind the plodding traditionalist that he must be a mature Catholic. Too long has he been spoon-fed like an infant on doctrinal pabulum. Now he is ready for strong meat. "Think for yourself!" And when the conservative who perhaps has grown gray in the Faith he loves, answers, "If I may think for myself, I stand where I was. I like it here," he is branded a helpless and hopeless conformist.

Even in the family circle, there is often a Catholic cleavage. The parents are horrified that the youngsters bring home heresies from parochial school or CCD. The children, on the other hand, shrug off their parents as not being with it, naive, pathetically behind the times.

There is something to be said, in all fairness, on both sides. The parents, perhaps, never realized that revealed religion did not come to us as a five-foot shelf of books complete with explanations, illustrations and diagrams. Considering the slow progress of mankind, it never should have. Even today there are millions of people who cannot read nor write. God, therefore, in the beginning had to transmit His truth by tradition, that is, by word of mouth. From generation to generation, religious truths were passed on in tales told by firelight. To help the memory, these truths were enshrined in stories, whose colorful details came from the local imagination, but the underlying truth was faithfully preserved.

In the story of Adam and Eve, for instance, what was important was not the apple nor the serpent, but that the human race had at one time rebelled against its Maker and had been punished for it. In the incident of the Three Kings or the Wise Men from the East, what mattered was not their names nor their number nor their rank, nor their origin, but that the good news of the Gospel was not for the Jews only, but for all nations.

In their way, then, the youngsters are correct, because the details of the stories are woven of rainbow poetry. But in their way, too, the parents need not worry: the underlying truths (and that is all that matters) are solid, stubborn steel.

What alarms some priests about the so-called new catechisms is that they find that the youngsters who have been exposed to them are strong on things like social justice, but weak on the sacraments, strong on community spirit but weak on Communion. But the catechism's purpose is primarily to teach the supernatural and go from there to the natural. Racial rights and help of the underprivileged, for instance, are never farther away than the parable of the Good Samaritan.

Perhaps we should all pray to Our Lady, Mother of the Church, as Pope Paul saluted her at the Vatican Council, to grant us two necessary virtues for these churning times. First, *Pazienza*, patience, so that we can survey the current scene calmly, knowing that since the Church has survived far worse, she will also survive this. And for just one reason: not that the clergy are particularly clever, not that the laity are especially pious, not because of Vatican diplomacy or financial wealth or political power, but simply and solely because the Church is the bark of Peter, and *Christ is aboard!*

Secondly, the virtue of charity. This means that we should give the Catholics who disagree with us credit for being as sincere as we are. Nothing drives people away from the Church like hatred. Nothing draws them closer than love.

A Broken Engagement

That broiling July, just thirty some years ago, a half-dozen of us knew that, barring a miracle, Helen would be dead before the winter's first blizzard. Even into the Fall, she herself never suspected. Her thoughts were mostly on Tom, a young fireman from Brookline, a town that abutted her own Boston. They had been keeping company, as the phrase then had it, for about six months. In their early twenties, they made a handsome pair, the vivacious dark-Irish type, and were deeply in love. The world, to be sure, was about to explode in the fiercest of all wars, but they were living in their own dream world. What they heard was not dive-bombers but bluebirds.

Then, quietly as the drift of a fog, a grave sickness came creeping over Helen. There was a twinge here and an ache there, and discomfort now and then, but mostly a loss of all energy, a weary, languishing weakness. So she went to one doctor, who sent her to another, and the report came back eventually that she had a hopeless variety of leukemia, or what the layman calls cancer of the blood.

The doctor told her parents. They told her two brothers, her boyfriend, and myself. We decided not to tell Helen for a while, and, as a matter of strange fact,

Tom, the boyfriend, kept on taking her out whenever she felt up to it, as if nothing were wrong. Later, of course, she had to take to her bed, and the time came to break the grim news. That day when I came into the sickroom in her home, Tom was kneeling beside the bed, his young eyes swimming in tears. He stumbled out, and I mentioned to Helen how I had often seen them together at the Wednesday night novena in honor of Our Mother of Perpetual Help. During the opening hymn, you could see from the pulpit many Romeos and Juliets hurrying down the aisles holding hands. It was not a bad preparation for the day when, arm in arm, a pair would walk down the aisle of their wedding.

A little table beside Helen's bed held a small picture of Our Mother of Perpetual Help, and when I picked it up she said, "You may not believe this, Father, but at the beginning of this week for three nights my mouth was on fire. I felt as if I had a mouthful of flame. Then I pressed Our Lady's picture to my lips, and from that moment all the burning stopped."

She was propped up in the bed and her wealth of long black hair made her pale face seem even whiter against the pillow. Her hollow eyes looked at me steadily as I shakily broke the news that she was gravely ill and that God might soon call her. It turned out not to be news at all. As in most cases, she had suspected something serious all along. So often the whole thing is a game of play-acting going on between the people around the bed and the patient in it. Each wants to make it easy for the other party.

And it was just one more occasion when the priest feels profoundly humble. He comes to console, and he leaves knowing that he has been on the receiving end of the inspiration and spiritual strength. Particularly with the young, this towering faith and deep resignation is a head-shaking wonder, all the more magnificent because all the more unexpected in the springtime of life, when they have so much to lose. So it was with Helen. In the darkness of that fatal sickness, her trust in God burned like a bright candle that illumined all who came near her. Because of the brave way she faced death, everybody around her felt influenced to live a better life.

But Helen was realistic, too. She smiled as if she were imagining a pleasant scene and said, "I suppose that if I could be healthy and spend my life with Tom, I'd want to live very much. God wants it this way, so, I accept. It must be the best, because He wants it." And then she said something that sounded deeper than you would expect, and she said it with a little incredulous shaking of her head: "You hear in sermons about this world being a tricky, shallow place, but you never believe it till you stand at the door and look around, just before you go out."

She went out that last door about two weeks later. She no longer needed the picture of Our Mother of Perpetual Help on her bedside table. The Mother of Perpetual Help *in person* was on the other side of the door waiting to welcome her to the heaven she deserved.

That was near Thanksgiving. A short time before Christmas, Tom came to the rectory one evening and laid a little plush box on the rectory table. I opened it and saw a slender, pretty ring with the bright sparkle of a diamond. Tom closed it quickly as if he could not bear the memory. His face was set and almost hardened in that stern sorrow that sits so strangely on the face of the young. "Three days before she died," he said, "she took it off and gave it back to me." He stopped as if he were seeing again the thin white finger and the ring spinning around it so loosely.

Then he bit his lip and went on. "That afternoon Helen said, 'Tom, I don't want my death to spoil your life. So I have said a prayer asking God to send the right girl into your life. You deserve a good girl. And when she comes, I want you to marry her and be happy. And when you become engaged, give her this ring.' "

"I tried to tell her," Tom went on, "that the last thing on my mind was another girl, and that if ever in the years to come one did come along, I certainly would never be able to slip *this* ring on her finger." He smiled. "You know, Father, Helen was practically dying and we were almost fighting."

"After a while she said, 'Many a night we went to the Wednesday novena at the Mission Church together. Some day they may have a new monstrance made for the Benedictions. Would you be willing to bring the ring to Father Manton and ask him to put it in that monstrance as a memorial of our beautiful love?' "

At the Mission Church we had not been thinking of a new monstrance, though we certainly could have used one, but one Wednesday soon afterward I did diffidently mention the possibility at all the eight services. Somewhere in their homes, I reminded them, in the dusty depths of old boxes or in the back of forgotten desk drawers, might lie sentimental pieces of jewelry, precious to them for more than their money value. Jewelry like this they could never bring themselves to sell, but they might be willing to see their keepsakes end up in a kind of Viking's funeral, melted down for Our Lady's monstrance.

The response roared back in a glittering golden stream of wedding rings and massive watches, bracelets and brooches, ear-rings and eye-glasses, Masonic emblems of converts and athletic medals of men who had long since broken the tape into eternity. Out of it all emerged a majestic monstrance, three feet tall, twelve pounds in weight, solid gold from base to tip, elegantly designed and encrusted with intricate clusters of diamonds.

For more than a quarter of a century, this monstrance has been raised at the Wednesday benedictions over the bowed heads in the benches, flashing like the revolving lamp of a slender, golden lighthouse. At the radio benediction each Wednesday, we pray that our Lord, who once walked the waves of the sea, will march across the airwaves into the homes of the shut-ins, even as He did at the first Easter, "the doors being shut."

The Novena devotions remind us that in one way Our Lady herself was the very first monstrance. True, she did not lift up a snow-white host, but at the crib of Bethlehem she did lift up the Child in white swaddling clothes, and perhaps sticks of straw clung to Him, like the golden rays of a monstrance, as He was raised in benediction over shepherds and kings.

Anyway, that's the history of our gold monstrance. I don't know which particular little diamond in it came from Helen's finger. I do know that all the rest are like jewelled tears from those that were touched by her story.

The Good Ole Summertime?

Some years ago a public relations man crossed the Alps on an elephant. It made historians smile because that stunt elephant was lumbering in the footsteps of his ancestors who had crossed the same Alps more than twenty centuries before. Those elephants were part of the pack train and the small picked army of Hannibal. How *he* ever crossed the Alps in mid-winter, climbing slippery mountain passes and fighting off hostile tribes along the way, is a mystery of history.

But at last he got to the other side of the mountain, and there below stretched the enchanting panorama of the soft green Italian spring. His soldiers cheered when they saw the lush valleys, the pretty groves, and above all, the warm golden sunshine. They found little difficulty conquering the inhabitants, and eventually reached the picturesque little city of Capua, set like a golden brooch in all the surrounding green.

Hannibal took Capua, but in a slyer sense Capua took Hannibal. The army that had cut its valiant way through mountain passes leaving blood upon the snow, now relaxed, like a vacationist lolling in a hammock. Soldiers of steel grew soft and became soldiers of satin and silk. When the enemy regrouped and attacked Capua, the soft soldiers of Hannibal found they had forgotten how to fight. The city fell, and many of the men who had crossed the Alps with such valor died in the massacre.

You may be thinking: all good enough, but what's Hannibal to me or me to Hannibal? Possibly, a grim and pertinent example for us all. Is not the history of Hannibal at Capua the history or the diary of some Catholics during the soft and leisurely summertime? There is a type of Catholic who in wintertime will trudge to Mass over crunching February snow, head bowed into a blizzard; but on vacation, when days are balmy and bright, he goes soft and skips Mass. At home he sometimes sees paperbacks on a drugstore rack, vile stuff that must have been written with a pen dipped in gore, putrid pages that ought to make a man's eyes vomit, and usually he would not touch such trash with a pair of tongs. Somehow on vacation his strong spiritual fiber goes limp and he dips into this paperback or that one, buys a couple, and soon muddy footprints have tracked across his mind.

This happens only on vacation. How do you explain it? Is it that men or women are like meat that stays wholesome in the cool refrigerator but becomes tainted and bad in summer heat? Can the devil grip a man's soul in the summertime the way a blacksmith's pincers grip a glowing hot horseshoe, and pound it into any shape he wants, whereas that man's metal, cold, would laugh at the blows of the hammer and give him back only a mocking tune? Is it not passing strange that "when the heat is on" both blacksmith and devil get better results?

A good deal of this happens at the seashore. During World War II, people used to shake their heads over the multitude of casualties on far-away beachheads, like Normandy, Tarawa, Anzio. But who will count the number of moral tragedies on our American beaches any year? The person who comes proudly striding home from the beach all healthy and bronzed may be spiritually limping and morally blackened or charred. There is a haunting line in the Gospel that says, "And when it was morning, there was Jesus standing on the shore." How sadly He stands, each summer, on some shores! In mid-September we keep the feast of the Sorrows of Mary. Liturgically we limit them to seven, but how many new sorrows are added yearly even by her own children?

For some the good old summertime turns out bad. For them it means less dress and more drink. They treat their conscience like the old time morning milk delivery where people used to drop a note in an empty bottle saying, "Going away for vacation. Won't be needing you for a while." Some Catholics when they "go away" become like the salamanders or chameleons sold at a circus, those tiny lizards that take on the color of their surroundings. Lay a chameleon on red, and the chameleon gradually turns red. Put it on green and it turns green. On plaid it might just go to pieces. That is what some Catholics do during vacation; they go to pieces. At least, like a chameleon, they take on the complexion of the company around them. If they find themselves surrounded by a crowd that is fast and loose, they become fast and loose.

Paste this in your vacation folder. Serious sin will spoil any summer. It does not matter where we go, whether we are lucky enough to be at a magic seashore where the beach wears the lapping white foam like a scalloped lace collar, or whether we are high in the mountains near a jewel-like lake cupped between emerald hills. It does not matter how serene or how gorgeous the background. Let serious sin enter the picture, and you have the serpent slithering into the lovely Garden of Eden, the arrival of evil that spoils everything.

It is so easy to deceive ourselves. On vacation everybody goes out for a good time. But it is not a good time to go away and leave religion behind and live as if there were no God. It is not a good time to spend a vacation daubing mud on the white tablets of the Ten Commandments. It is not a good time to pass the summer in a moral graveyard, dancing on the grave of a dead soul, dancing on buried virtue, dancing on moral corruption. When the day is over, and the music has stopped, and the laughter is stilled, and you lie in your dark room looking up at the ceiling, then you will know "who is kidding whom," and you will find that a human heart studded with sin is a heavy load for anyone to bear.

And who wants to carry the burden of guilt? The Church wants us to be happy. She wants us to have rest, relaxation, recreation, change. She is no sour gloom-artist, no vinegar-faced killjoy, always frowning on fun, shaking a threatening finger and snapping, "Nice children don't *do* that!" She wants us to be happy within the boundaries of the only place where we can be happy — the solid and sensible law of God. Nobody, not even the Church, can dispense from that, in July or in January. She can no more repeal the law of God during the summer than she can suspend the law of gravity. Let us therefore be good as well as happy, and put the emphasis on the backbone as well as on the funnybone.

One way to insure a summer that will not lure us away from God is to be loyal to our devotion in honor of His Holy Mother. If we stay close to her, we shall never stray far from Him.

Two Masters

One somber November afternoon a few years ago, when the wind burbled like an Indian war-cry and the sharp cold cut you like a knife, a souvenir vendor stood outside a football stadium crying his wares. He wore a battered brown hat and a long shabby grey overcoat. The left side of the coat from tightly buttoned collar down to the frayed bottom was bright with tiny gilt footballs sporting the ribbons of Boston College. The right side glittered with the same rows of little footballs but these carried the fluttering ribbons of Holy Cross. Similarly, his left arm offered a bundle of pennants in the maroon and gold of Boston College, while the right arm held just as many of Holy Cross' purple and white. All the while he shouted "B.C.! Holy Cross! Holy Cross! B.C.!" He was the perfect picture of neutrality, the absolute image of impartiality. Solomon's sword could have split him straight down the middle and handed one side to Boston College and the other to its arch-rival, Holy Cross.

He could be neutral because he was serving the almighty dollar. But no man can be neutral if he is trying to serve Almighty God. Here is one area where we cannot divide our allegiance for any reason whatever. In other departments compromise is possible. They say that you cannot carry water on both shoulders, but in the Orient, thanks to two buckets and a pole, that is the way they do carry it. They say you cannot burn the candle at both ends, but according to the poet that is precisely when "it gives a lovely light." They say you cannot keep people's respect if you are a turncoat, but in these days of reversible raincoats you can not only be respectable but even fashionable. However when we deal with God, semantics will not help. We must serve either Him or Mammon, God or the World.

One of the sternest and strangest phrases that fell from the lips of Christ (and this was at the banquet of love the night before He died) was this: "For the world I do not pray." It has the grim finality of a turned back, of a closed door, even of a lid being lowered on a casket. Our Lord, to be sure, meant the *spirit* of the world, and some of us may conjecture that from century to century the spirit of the world changes. If it does, it changes only the way a snake changes its skin. Ever so often the snake gets a new skin but never a different skin. It is always the same slick and slimy stripes.

The tapes of nineteen centuries are filed away in the vault of time since Christ died, and has the spirit of the world changed so much? Is it not still a world with shrugging unbelief in its head, grabbing materialism in its hands, corroding lust in its heart? Here for example in our own United States it is a world where half the people do not darken the door of a church on Sunday morning. The chimes of the church bells are drowned out by the rustle of the Sunday papers, and Christ cannot compete with the comics. It is a world where they piously put "In God we trust" on coins and then pay less heed to some of His commandments than to the "Keep off the grass" signs in the park. It is a world where in the sacred contract of matrimony the words "till death do us part" have lost so much prestige that now an option to divorce almost comes with the marriage license, like a raincheck with a baseball ticket.

It is a world where graft is not stealing, so long as the gravy is lapped up quietly. It is a world where the heroes and heroines of our young people are taken from stage and screen, while the real *moving* pictures, the pictures of the saints, are relegated to art museums where people who do not believe in saints prowl past them with guidebooks, perish the thought of prayerbooks! It is a world where schoolteachers can expound on Venus, the pagan goddess who gave her name to venereal disease, but dare not discuss the Virgin Mary who has been the sweetest symbol and the strongest influence for chastity that this earth has ever known. It is a world where the code calls for respectability but not for morality; meaning that anything goes as long as it goes on behind the closed venetian blinds of privacy. As long as you are not found out and there is no scandal, then there is no sin, no guilt, no shame, and everything is roses.

This would be true only if there were no God. And the truth is, not that there is no God but that He is forgotten. Ordinary good persons who hear His Gospel for so short a time each Sunday, are bombarded with the gospel of the world the whole rest of the week, from paperbacks and billboards, from newspapers and television and radio and the rest. That is why it is important that we constantly remind ourselves that our Lord was miraculously born in Bethlehem, performed astounding wonders in Judea, died for us on Calvary, rose on the third day as He had promised, founded His Church to help us reach heaven, and will one day be our final Judge. It is to neutralize the spirit of the world all about us that such little things as morning and evening prayers are important, along with such great things as Holy Mass and the Sacraments. They all help us to remember to serve one Master even in a hostile world.

Some men try to take a leaf from Roman history and try to compromise by turning the human heart into a Pantheon. In the original Pantheon every pagan god had its pedestal — thundering Jupiter and helmeted Mars and winged Mercury and all the others. But even the "broadminded" Romans would not invite into their fantastic collection the God of the Christians, because they knew He would permit no false gods before Him. Yet there are Christians today who want God in the temple of their heart but who also want other little altars there, dedicated to hate or lust or revenge or avarice or gambling or drink, so that it becomes a Pantheon of Passions. They forget that God will still brook no rivals.

Curiously, the Roman Pantheon is even now remarkably well preserved. For many centuries it has been a Christian church dedicated to St. Mary of the Martyrs. There is a neat symbolism here, because those who turn out evil passions from their heart and give it over to Jesus and Mary, have to be martyrs themselves to constant restraint and courageous self-control.

It is always so easy to fall for the phony philosophy of the world. It is so easy for instance for parents to make sure that their youngster gets enough vitamins and yet pay little attention to the development of his virtues. It is so easy for a young man going out on a date to select a snappy, immaculate shirt and then return from the date with the shirt still crisp and clean but his conscience smudged and soiled. It is so easy for a young girl to be tempted to put aside the white flower of purity and to pin on the scarlet blossom of popularity, which is so often bold and cheap and soon ends up a pitiful thing, crumpled by many hands, and hanging its head in secret bitter shame. No man, and no woman either, can serve two masters. It has to be, in the scriptural scale, either God or the world.

There is no half-way house between. We cannot swing between the trapezes of virtue and sin, because beneath us there is no saving circus net but only the fires of hell. We have to make our choice. We have to take our stand. We have to be counted with Christ or against Him. There is no place for compromise, only for total commitment. No man can serve two masters. But we can all serve one, and serve Him well, if we have good will on our part and sustaining grace on His.

2456 1